DISCARD

NELSON AND WINNIE MANDELA

NELSON
—— AND ——
WINNIE
MANDELA

DOROTHY
AND THOMAS
HOOBLER

Franklin Watts/1987
New York/London/Toronto/Sydney
An Impact Biography

Library of Congress Cataloging-in-Publication Data
Hoobler, Dorothy.
Nelson and Winnie Mandela
(An impact biography)
Bibliography: p.
Includes index.
Summary: Presents the lives and careers of the
imprisoned leader of the African National Congress
and his wife, an activist in the struggle for
black majority rights in South Africa.
1. Mandela, Nelson, 1918–   —Juvenile literature.
2. Mandela, Winnie—Juvenile literature.   3. Civil
rights workers—South Africa—Biography—Juvenile
literature.   4. South Africa—Race relations—Juvenile
literature.   5. African National Congress—Juvenile
literature.   [1. Mandela, Nelson, 1918–
2. Mandela, Winnie.   3. Civil rights workers—South
Africa.   4. Blacks—Biography.   5. African National
Congress]   I. Hoobler, Thomas.   II Title.
DT779.95.M36H67 1987   323.4'092'2 [B] [92]   86-26631
ISBN 0-531-10332-3

CONTENTS

This book is for the two Ellens:
one born in the month
the Statue of Liberty
was first dedicated,
the other born in the
year of the Bicentennial.

CHAPTER

1

A MEMBER
OF THE
ROYAL HOUSE

As a child, Nelson Mandela loved to sit in the circle of people around a fire, listening to the tribal elders tell stories of the brave deeds of the African warriors who were his ancestors. The elders described the way life had been in Africa before the coming of Europeans. It was a time, Nelson later recalled, when "our people lived peacefully, under the democratic rule of their kings and their councillors, and moved freely and confidently up and down the country without let or hindrance. Then the country was ours...we occupied the land, the forests, the rivers; we extracted the mineral wealth beneath the soil and all the riches of this beautiful country. We set up and operated our own government, we controlled our own armies, and we organized our own trade and commerce."

The elders told of the wars fought by Nelson's ancestors to defend their homeland. The young boy thrilled to hear of the acts of bravery performed by the tribal warriors during those days of glory.

By the time Nelson was born, those days existed only in memory. Nelson grew up in a world where white Europeans had taken control of the land. Yet the stories of

Nelson's youth were to act as an inspiration to him. He was to devote his life to trying to recover the rights of his people.

Nelson Rolihlahla Mandela was born on July 18, 1918, at Qunu, near Umtata, the capital of the Transkei reserve in the southeastern part of South Africa. The Transkei is a land of hilly grasslands and woods. To the east lies the sea; to the west lie the mountains.

Nelson was a member of the royal family of the Thembu, a Xhosa-speaking people who were one of many black African groups in this part of the continent. He was the eldest son of Henry Gadla Mandela and one of his four wives, Nonqaphi. Henry was the chief councillor to the Paramount Chief of the Thembu people, and Nonqaphi was recognized as a woman of dignity. Nelson's Xhosa name, Rolihlahla, was prophetic. It means "stirring up trouble."

Nelson's father had been among the black volunteers who served with British troops in South-West Africa against the Germans in World War I. Henry was a respected elder who served on the Transkeian Territories General Council, known as the Bunga, which advised the government in Pretoria on local matters.

The whitewashed huts of the family *kraal*, or farm, were the setting for Nelson's childhood. Like the other children, he helped to herd the cattle and sheep and plow the fields.

Although neither of his parents was educated in the Western sense, Nelson had a keen desire for learning. He was enrolled at a local school run by white missionaries. Friends from that time recall that the other students teased him because of his shabby clothing. It must have been a blow to his pride, but Nelson persevered. He applied himself diligently to his first contact with such unfamiliar things as reading, writing, and elementary arithmetic. His hunger for knowledge was to stay with him throughout his life.

SOUTH AFRICA

ZIMBABWE

MOZAMBIQUE

SWAZILAND

INDIAN
OCEAN

BOTSWANA

Transvaal

Pretoria

Johannesburg

Soweto

Sharpeville

Orange Free State

Natal

Durban

LESOTHO

Umtata

Transkei

Pondoland

SOUTH
AFRICA

Brandfort

NAMIBIA

Windhoek

Cape of Good Hope

Uitenhage

ATLANTIC
OCEAN

Cape Town

ROBBINS ISLAND

*Transskei, in south-
eastern South Africa*

A scene in Umtata,
the capital of Transkei

When Nelson was twelve, Henry Mandela became ill. He presented his son to the Paramount Chief, saying, "I am giving you this servant, Rolihlahla. I can say from the way he speaks to his sisters and friends that his inclination is to help the nation. I want you to make him what you would like him to be. Give him education; he will follow your example."

Nelson went to live with the Paramount Chief in the Chief's Great Place. Here he was brought up with the chief's son, David Sabata Dalindyebo, and the brothers Kaiser and George Matanzima, who were close relatives of Nelson's. The Matanzima brothers were in later years to take different political paths from the one Nelson followed.

At the age of sixteen, Nelson prepared for his circumcision ceremony. With other young men of his age group, he retired to the mountains, painting his face white and wearing the traditional grass skirt. There tribal elders prepared the youth for the rites of manhood and for participation in the tribal councils.

Nelson was fascinated by the tribal courts, at which elders served as judges. The tribal courts regulated traditional African life. The central government allowed them to keep order in African areas. They were not associated with the central government.

Nelson loved to listen to the judges question and cross-examine witnesses. Afterward, they came to a judgment with the help of a tribal council. It was from this experience that Nelson developed a respect for the law. Few could have guessed that this respect would develop into an ambition to be a lawyer in the great white city of Johannesburg.

Nelson's traditional childhood had insulated him from the condition of other black Africans in the country. In the Cape Province, African property-holders had been allowed to vote in elections since 1854. Blacks believed that through education, more of them would meet the property require-

The hut at the Great Place
where Nelson Mandela lived
in the 1920s and 1930s

ments so that eventually all blacks would be granted full citizenship in the country. Nelson's grandfather had donated land for a mission school, so that his people could be educated for citizenship.

Then, in the mid-1930s, while Nelson was preparing for a Methodist high school, black Africans were dismayed to learn that the parliament in Cape Town had removed black voters from the rolls of eligible voters. The discriminatory laws that already applied in the other provinces were extended to the Cape Province.

Nelson began to examine the reasons why blacks in South Africa were second-class citizens in their own country. He had to learn the history of white settlement in South Africa.

Eight years before Nelson's birth, the Union of South Africa had been created from the British and Dutch territories of southern Africa. This was the culmination of a series of struggles between these two European peoples for supremacy in southern Africa.

The Dutch settlers, known as Boers, had arrived before the British. In 1652, the Dutch East India Company had established a colony at the Cape of Good Hope, on the southern tip of the continent. The Dutch settlers encountered the Khoi-Khoi people (Hottentots) and the San (Bushmen). These were Africans who had been driven south by the ancestors of Nelson's people.

By the end of the century, more Dutch, and a sprinkling of French Huguenots and Germans, had arrived. They brought with them black and Malay slaves. Intermarriage between these white and black immigrants produced a group of people who were called Cape Coloreds. By the end of the eighteenth century, the Cape of Good Hope was a thriving colony.

In 1806, the British took the colony from the Dutch. Soon British settlers began to arrive, and when slavery was abolished throughout the British Empire in 1834, the blacks in South Africa were freed. To the Boer farmers, this meant an unacceptable change in their way of life. Economically, the farmers were dependent on slave labor.

A great number of Boers set out on a journey to the north, away from British influence. They traveled in small groups with their slaves, carrying their possessions in ox-drawn wagons. The Boers were a religious but tough people. Each wagon held both a Bible and a rifle. They believed they were fulfilling a divine destiny for their people. This mass migration of the Boers became known as the Great Trek, and is celebrated in memorials by the Boers' descendants, today's Afrikaners.

To the Boers, the sign of God's blessing on their purpose came in 1838, when they encountered about twelve thousand Zulu warriors at the Ncome River in what is today's Natal Province. The Boers formed a *laager* by drawing their wagons into a circle. As the Zulus attacked with their spears, the Boers' rifles mowed them down. The river turned red with the blood of the slain, and today is known as Blood River.

In commemoration of the victory, the Boers erected a church on the battle site. In South Africa today, the date of the battle is celebrated in December as the Day of the Covenant.

Yet the British, whose military power was greater than that of the Boers, soon followed the Boers northward, extending British rule over Natal. The British built sugarcane plantations there, and to work them brought a new element into South Africa's complicated mix of people. These were indentured laborers and free immigrants from India.

In response to the British expansion, the Boers moved farther inland, to the high veldt, a grassy plateau. The Boers set up two states, the Orange Free State and the Transvaal. Here, too, the Boers subjugated the black African population. The British recognized the independence of the Boer states in the 1850s, and for a time, the two European peoples coexisted in an uneasy peace.

Then, in 1867, diamonds were discovered in northern Cape Province. Nine years later, a large gold strike was made in the Transvaal. Land that had been thought useful only as farmland now became a rich prize. Prospectors poured in from all over the world. European capitalists bought up land to develop the mineral resources. The diamond capital, Kimberley, and Johannesburg, the center of the gold-mining industry, mushroomed into major cities. Railroads were built from the Cape, bringing a new influx of foreigners.

The Boers regarded all this as a threat to their way of life. Tensions increased between the British and Afrikaner regions. The result was the arrival of a British military force, and the outbreak of the Boer War (1899–1902). The British treated the Boers with great brutality, burning their farms to drive them off the land. When the Boer men formed commando groups to resist, the British rounded up their women and children and put them into camps in the South. For the first time, the world heard the term "concentration camps." Disease and famine raged in the camps, and thousands of Boers died because of neglect and ill-treatment.

Many blacks supported the British forces, some for pay, some out of principle, because the British treated them better than the Boers had. In addition, the British government assured the blacks that they would eventually receive the same rights and privileges as whites.

The British triumphed in the Boer War, but the scars left by their victory remained for generations. In the Treaty of Vereeniging (1902) that ended the war, a decision about voting rights for the black Africans was postponed until the colony should be granted self-government. A colonial official in London remarked, "The natives will never have the franchise. No responsible government will give it to them."

He was right. In 1910, the Union of South Africa was established from the Cape Province, Natal, the Orange Free

State, and the Transvaal. At the same time, the British tried to make amends for their brutal treatment of the Boers. They did so at the expense of the black South Africans. Although South Africa was to be part of the British Commonwealth, the decision as to who could vote was left to the four separate provincial legislatures. Most of these were dominated by Afrikaners, descendants of the Boer settlers. These legislatures soon began to pass restrictive legislation against blacks.

Among these laws was the requirement that male blacks carry a government-issued pass. Essentially, this requirement was to ensure that the whites could control the movements of blacks in white areas. A certain number of blacks were needed to do menial jobs that whites were unwilling to do, but the Afrikaners wanted to make sure that the majority of blacks stayed in the rural areas. However, the restrictions were enforced more strictly in some places than in others.

As Nelson Mandela grew to young manhood, educational opportunities were still open to blacks in South Africa. In 1936, he enrolled in Fort Hare College, a Methodist college in eastern Cape Province that was to become a training ground for African leaders. Here he met Oliver Tambo, today the leader of the African National Congress in exile. They were to be lifelong friends and political allies. Tambo recalls that Nelson was sensitive and quick to resent any slight, but at the same time popular with the other students.

It was at Fort Hare that Nelson's political education began. After three years of study, he was suspended from the school for joining a boycott of the Students' Representative Council, to which he had been elected. The boycott had been called because the school had stripped the council of its power.

Nelson returned to his home in the Transkei. The Paramount Chief was not pleased at Nelson's suspension. He urged Nelson to cooperate with the school authorities.

In addition, Nelson recalled, "My guardian felt it was time for me to get married. He loved me very much and looked after me as diligently as my father had. But he was no democrat and did not think it worthwhile to consult me about a wife. He selected a girl, fat and dignified; *lobola* [bride-price] was paid, and arrangements were made for the wedding."

To avoid the arranged marriage, Nelson left, heading for Johannesburg, the largest city in South Africa.

Johannesburg had begun as a gold-mining boom town in the heart of the Transvaal. Among the nationalities who poured into the region in the 1880s were Australians, Americans, Russian Jews, and English. Though the Transvaal was the center of the Boer nation, Johannesburg took on a cosmopolitan character that was entirely foreign to the culture of the religious Boer farmers. The Boer leader, Paul Kruger, called it Buiwelstad, "the devil's town." To black Africans, it was known as Egoli, "the city of gold."

When Nelson arrived, he worked for a time in the gold mines around the city, and later took other odd jobs. For the first time, he experienced the horrendous conditions in which the blacks lived in white-ruled South Africa. The "Bantus"—the white term for all black Africans—lived in slum areas, known as townships, on the outskirts of the city. Without electricity or sewage facilities, ramshackle houses were crowded next to one another in filthy surroundings. Like Nelson, many of the blacks living in the townships had come from the countryside in search of work.

In Johannesburg, Nelson had to carry a government-issued pass at all times. He could be stopped by the police for any reason and required to show his pass. It was im-

Nelson Mandela
at age nineteen

possible to get work without one, and the pass also showed where the holder was permitted to live. If a black obtained a job within the white area of the city, a special stamp showed permission to be in the area. The white employer had to sign the pass each month. If any aspect of the pass was not in order, the holder could be immediately sent back to the countryside. Blacks could suffer the loss of their pass for any act that might be interpreted as rudeness toward a white. Normally, they were required to step off the sidewalk when a white passed by.

Conditions for black Africans had worsened after passage of the Natives Land Act in 1913. The act set aside 7.3 percent of South Africa's total area for ownership and use by blacks. A census two years earlier had shown that there were 4 million blacks in the country, compared with 1.25 million whites and 600,000 Cape Coloreds and Indians.

Though by far the majority in the country, blacks remained powerless to achieve the political representation or the equality their numbers demanded. Though powerless, they were not passive. Two years after the establishment of the Union of South Africa, in 1912, four black African lawyers founded the group that became the African National Congress (ANC). Its aim was to unite the African people—who had traditionally been divided against one another by tribal rivalries—to fight white domination. One of the founders of the ANC said, "We must think in wider political terms, for we are one people." The members of the ANC set out to remove the legal forms of discrimination against blacks.

Top: Johannesburg, 1976
Bottom: Squatter's camp near
the black township of Cross-
roads, near Cape Town, 1983

Nelson arrived in Johannesburg during World War II. Though black Africans had volunteered to serve, they were not allowed in combat positions; they served in the army, as in the rest of white society, as menial laborers.

However, the war had drawn many Europeans into the armed services. Thus, a few better-than-usual jobs were available for blacks within the city.

Nelson settled in the township of Alexandra. A neighbor told him to get in touch with Walter Sisulu. Sisulu owned a small real-estate agency in the city and promptly offered Nelson a job. Theirs was to be a fateful meeting for the future of the black struggle.

The two men became friends. Nelson confided in Sisulu his dream of studying law. Sisulu saw in the young man qualities that should be encouraged. He helped Nelson obtain his college degree through a correspondence course.

Though many laws discriminated against blacks, conditions were not so bad at this time as they would become after the establishment of the apartheid system in 1948. Many whites opposed the racist policy of the government, and some careers were open to blacks that would be forbidden later. After Nelson completed his studies, Sisulu introduced him to a firm of white lawyers. They offered Nelson a job in their office, and sponsored his admission to law studies at the nearby University of Witwatersrand.

For Nelson, the experience at the law firm gave him his first social contact with whites. In his earlier experiences, the whites he had known were teachers, traders, and judges. His new employers considered themselves enlightened people. The head typist told him, "We have no color bar here. When the teaboy brings the tea, come and get yours from the tray."

However, two new cups had been bought for the special use of Nelson and an Indian clerk, Gaur Radebe. As Nelson recalled it, Radebe was an arrogant little man, "politically radical." In the matter of the cups, he told Nelson, "You watch and do exactly as I do." When the tea was passed around, Radebe ignored his designated cup and took one of the old ones. Embarrassed and shy, Nelson explained that he did not drink tea.

Nelson found it hard to complete his duties at the firm, take the long train ride to the university, and return home in time for the curfew that applied to blacks. One of the partners in the firm encouraged him to persevere. He told Nelson that by becoming a good lawyer he could earn "the respect of all sections of the population." However, the partner advised, he should avoid politics. That was one piece of advice Nelson did not take.

In Johannesburg, he met and married Evelyn Ntoko Mase, a nurse at the City Deep Mine Hospital. They set up a home in Orlando, one of the expanding black townships. Near them lived Walter Sisulu and his wife Albertina. Soon Oliver Tambo arrived in Johannesburg and met his old friend from Fort Hare College. Through Nelson and Walter Sisulu he soon became involved in the black political struggle.

Walter Sisulu was already a member of the African National Congress. He brought Nelson and Oliver Tambo to one of the meetings, and they enrolled as members. At this time, the early enthusiasm raised by the Congress had faded in the face of opposition and indifference. These three young men were to rejuvenate the organization and change the course of the African nationalist movement in South Africa.

CHAPTER

2

DEVISING
A POLITICAL
STRATEGY

Nelson joined the African National Congress in 1944. The humiliating conditions imposed on blacks had made a deep impression on him. His desire to change their status had brought him to join the Congress, and in its work he found a goal that gave shape and meaning to his life. From that time to the present, he has been involved in the struggle on behalf of black Africans in South Africa. He has never deviated from the goal of furthering the rights of his people.

Yet in spite of his political commitment, he always kept his striking human qualities—a strong sense of humor, an interest in other people, a buoyancy of outlook in the face of hardship, and devotion to his friends. His friend Oliver Tambo described him this way: "He has the natural air of authority. He cannot help magnetizing a crowd: he is commanding, with a tall, handsome bearing; trusts and is trusted by the youth, for their impatience reflects his own; appealing to the women. He is dedicated and fearless. He is the born mass leader."

When Mandela joined the Congress, the organization had lost some of the vigor of its early days. Many blacks believed that it had accomplished little. Its efforts to remove the color bar in parliament, education, and industry had shown few results. The government had responded to the peaceable demonstrations organized by the Congress only with violence and further repression. In the 1920s and 1930s, as more blacks became part of the industrial and mining work force of the country, the Industrial and Commercial Workers Union (ICU) took much of the initiative from the ANC in the struggle for black rights. The ICU organized workers for strikes to protest poor working conditions and low wages.

Mandela, Sisulu, and Tambo set out to revitalize the African National Congress. They were determined to change the ANC from "a body of gentlemen with clean hands" to an organization that would be more effective in challenging the policies of the South African government. Along with others, they helped form a Youth League within the ANC.

In one statement of their philosophy, they declared: "The Congress Youth League must be the brains-trust and power-station of the spirit of African nationalism; the spirit of African self-determination; the spirit that is so discernible in the thinking of our youth. It must be an organization where young African men and women will meet and exchange ideas in an atmosphere pervaded by a common hatred of oppression."

They saw their role as "galvanizing" the ANC, which they recognized as "the symbol and embodiment of the African's will to present a united front against all forms of oppression." They recognized that the weaknesses of the group in the past had led to the creation of rival organizations. However, they stressed the need for a united group that would become politically sophisticated.

The ANC's membership had previously consisted of the best-educated blacks. The leaders of the Youth League intended to make a greater effort to reach the great majority of the African people. They declared their intention to rouse "popular political consciousness and [to fight] oppression." The Youth League "will educate the people politically by concentrating its energies on the African home front to make all sections of our people Congress-minded and nation-conscious."

The beginning of World War II in Europe in 1939 served as a stimulus to the Youth League's organizing efforts. During World War II, South Africa fought on the side of the Allies, against Germany. Many black Africans volunteered to serve in the war effort. As one leader of the ANC put it: "The country is in danger. Even if a man has quarreled with his wife, when he sees an enemy approaching his home, he gets up to settle with that enemy."

The war against Nazism abroad stimulated the desire for freedom at home. Although the South African government forbade Africans to strike, there were several strikes during the war. In another action, people in Alexandra, a black township outside Johannesburg, boycotted the bus service to protest a rise in the bus fare. Even though it was midwinter, thousands walked to work rather than pay. After nine days, the bus fare was reduced.

In 1945, after the Allied victory in World War II, the ANC took part in the victory march in Johannesburg—the biggest parade that the city had seen. Twenty thousand Africans followed a marching band, waving the ANC flag of black (for the people), green (for the land), and gold (for the wealth of their country). Their slogan was "Let's finish the job!"

In 1946, the struggle for civil rights in South Africa shifted to the Indian population. Most of the Indians were descended from those who had come to work on the sugar plantations in Natal in the nineteenth century. Though many Indians had prospered—some now owned shops and businesses—they, like the blacks and the Cape Coloreds, were relegated to second-class status by South African law.

Earlier in the century, Mohandas Gandhi, then a young lawyer in South Africa, had organized his first "passive resistance" campaign to protest the government's mistreatment of Indians in the country. Later, he would employ this same technique to win independence for India itself.

After World War II, the South African government decided that the Indian population was to be segregated in certain areas. The Indians organized protests; their efforts were supported financially by fellow Indians in their home country. One of the leaders of the demonstration was Ismail Meer, a fellow student with Nelson at Witwatersrand University. The two had become friends, and Nelson frequently stayed at Ismail's apartment. Although the Indian resistance campaign took place in the east coast city of Durban, much of the planning took place in Johannesburg.

Mandela was impressed with the Indians' dedication and hard work. Attending the planning sessions over curry and tea in Ismail's apartment was an exhilarating experience for him. It was his first experience with a successful protest against the government.

Nevertheless, Nelson remained convinced that Africans must lead their own movement; he retained a certain suspicion of "foreign" influences. He was particularly uneasy with the number of communists who supported the Indian protest. Meer described Nelson as "violently anti-communist," mainly because of Nelson's strong belief in Christianity.

The South African Communist Party was the only white party willing to work with Africans, and it had drawn support from some African nationalists. Even so, when Nelson was asked to join the party, he refused.

In 1946, black African mine workers organized a strike. Seven of Johannesburg's mines were shut down; an estimated 70,000 workers joined the strike. It was a serious threat to the economy of a country so dependent on its gold and diamond mines. The government responded by sealing off the workers' living quarters. Then police with rifles and batons forced the men back to work. Some workers were killed, and the strike was broken.

A scene at the historic mine workers' conference at Newtown Market Square, Johannesburg, on August 4. At the microphone is Mr. James Majoro, secretary of the African Mine Workers' Union, standing between two interpreters. The president, Mr. J. B. Marks, is standing on the left.

PRESS GO ON PASS RAIDS

PRETORIA — The police have become so alarmed over the outburst of criticism following recent "pass raids" on local locations that for their latest nocturnal raids they actually invited representatives of the daily Press. The bag that evening was a little lower than average, being about 250 Africans variously described as "vagrants," "illegal residents" and "wanted criminals."

Everything was above board according to the "Rand Daily Mail" report. At 4 a.m. the police knocked politely on house doors "with their batons" until the occupants awoke. "Tactful persuasion," he wrote, "was the keynote of the raid."

Police officials state that more frequent raids are to follow.

COUNCILLOR MRS. Z. GOOL

DURBAN — Councillor Mrs. Z. Gool, of Cape Town, was among the resisters arrested on Monday night. She was sentenced to 30 days' hard labour. Mrs. Gool has done great work for Passive Resistance in an intensive campaign in the Transvaal and Natal, at which she addressed many crowded meetings.

GENERAL BARKER No. 1 JEW-BAITER

CAPE TOWN. The vilely anti-Semitic tone of the news reports in the daily Press, the mud-slinging at the courageous and resourceful underground workers who are trying to rescue Jews still imprisoned in concentration camps, is unpleasantly reminiscent of Goebbels at his worst. The British Government seems to be usurping the role lately occupied by the Nazis as No. 1 Jew-baiters. Below we publish a report from "The Week" of London, which confirms this:

The War Office, the Colonial Office and indeed the Cabinet itself have been in a pretty considerable flap throughout the week over the Barker utterances on Palestine.

Because quite apart from the natural and almost universal disgust at the rabidly anti-Semitic tone of the Barker order — and people in London are saying that nothing quite as typical of the Streicher mentality has been produced since Streicher himself went out of commission — a whole series of strange and altogether less admirable reactions have been provoked up and down Whitehall.

The red face of the War Office has appeared to be redder than usual in the course of the week, because, whatever excuses may be offered and many are being offered just now, the fact remains that General Barker's forceful views on the J.'s have always been perfectly well known to anyone who has had the remotest connection with him.

And whatever they could deny, the War Office have been unable to deny their responsibility for transferring Barker from the command of our forces in Schleswig-Holstein to his present job in Palestine.

The Colonial Office and the Cabinet, of course, are far from pleased that our top-ranking man on the spot should make the sort of statement just now which will make the unpopular British policy in Palestine even more unpopular than it was before. And in this connection they have been watching American reaction to Barker with the very closest attention.

It is one thing for the British Commander-in-Chief to express his strongly anti-Semitic views in private. But to talk in an official order about "punishing the Jew in a way that the race dislikes — by hitting at their pockets and showing our contempt for them" is the Colonial Office's idea of carrying a good thing too far. And there is reason to believe that inter-departmental sparks have already begun to fly.

The only people in Government and Parliamentary circles who were not shocked into silence, of course, were those who have been in Palestine recently and know something of the views of Barker and many of his officers on the Jews.

It has been open talk among these people for some time that Barker was anti-Semitic and that his anti-Semitism has in fact spread to an alarming extent throughout the Army in Palestine. And Barker would find it difficult to deny that he said on a recent occasion that in his opinion "all the bloody Yids should be cleared out of Palestine."—(The Week.)

TWO MILLION U.S. TROOPS IN CHINA

Nearly 2,000 civilians have been killed and injured by air-raids with American war planes, which have made 810 sorties since last January's truce was broken by the Kuomintang.

It is revealed there are over 200,000 American troops, including marines, airmen, and all arms in China to-day.—D. & O.N.

GREATEST STRIKE IN S.A. HISTORY

MORE THAN 50,000 OUT

JOHANNESBURG — On Tuesday morning the African Mineworkers' Union office was raided by police. All documents, records of membership cards were seized. The police produced a search warrant, on suspicion that an "offence" had been committed.

On Wednesday morning the capitalist Press announced that "the first evidence" had been found linking the Union with the strike! They ignore the fact that on August 4, at meetings called by the Union and attended by delegates from most mines, it was agreed to strike on August 12 unless the workers' demands were met. THIS DECISION WAS WIDELY PUBLICISED BY THE UNION AND PUBLISHED IN THE PRESS CONTROLLED BY THE MINE-OWNERS AS WELL AS IN THE GUARDIAN.

The President of the Union, Mr. J. B. Marks (who is an African and not a Coloured man as the capitalist Press incorrectly reports) has been arrested. Another arrest is that of Mr. Ben Siachy, a prominent member of the Council for Asiatic Rights.

A committee of four Cabinet Ministers — Mines (Mr. S. F. Waterson), Labour (Dr. Colin Steyn), Justice (Mr. H. G. Lawrence), Native Affairs (Major P. van der Byl) — has been appointed by the Prime Minister "to deal with the strike."

THEIR JOB IS AN EASY ONE. LET THEM FORCE THE MINE-OWNERS TO NEGOTIATE WITH THE AFRICAN MINE-WORKERS' UNION, WHICH REPRESENTS THE WORKERS. THIS IS WHAT EVERY TRADE UNIONIST AND EVERY DEMOCRAT IN SOUTH AFRICA MUST DEMAND. (African Mineworkers' Union Statement: Page five)

JOHANNESBURG. On Tuesday morning, the police, bearing search warrants, raided the office of the African Mine Workers' Union and confiscated nearly all the documents, records and other papers. Mr. J. B. Marks, president of both the African Mine Workers' Union and the Transvaal Council of Non-European Trade Unions, has been arrested on a charge under the Riotous Assemblies Act. Mr. E. B. Mofutsanyana, editor of "Inkululeko," who was visiting the union office as a journalist, was taken to Marshall Square and kept there for five hours by the police for questioning, without any charge being made against him.

Despite unparalleled police violence and frantic propaganda efforts the whole week, between 45,000 and 50,000 African miners on the Witwatersrand struck work on Monday morning, demanding 10s. a day minimum wage and improved conditions.

Telegram to Smuts

The following telegram has been sent to the Prime Minister by Mr. W. H. Andrews, the National Chairman of the S.A. Communist Party:

National Executive of Communist Party condemns use of police terrorism with resultant deaths to break strike of mine workers for the right to live stop We demand your Government immediately end police intimidation and compel mine owners to negotiate with African Mine Workers' Union.

A news blackout was at first imposed by the capitalist press, but as the strike spread in response to the strike decision on the East Rand the newspapers were forced to admit the strike was on.

The New Kleinfontein and Robinson Deep miners came out 100 per cent. All or part of the African labour force are now on strike at the following mines: Brakpan, State Mines, Springs, West Springs, Van Dyk, City Deep, Marievale, Modder B. Nourse Mines, Van Ryn Estates, Vlakfontein, Simmer and Jack, Sub Nigel, Witwatersrand Gold Mine.

At New Kleinfontein three men were arrested on Monday. Eight thousand workers marched to the Benoni police station, demanding their release. A tense situation resulted with armed police standing at the gates of the police station with fixed bayonets, refusing to allow the strikers to enter.

POLICE TERRORISM

There are reports of exceptional measures by the police at West Rand to prevent strike action. City Deep, Robinson Deep and Randfontein report large forces of police were rushed from Johannesburg and serious violence was used against the workers.

It is stated in the capitalist press this police terrorism and baton charges against the strikers was on instructions from Pretoria.

The "Rand Daily Mail" on Monday, under the headline "Attempt to force Native Mine Strike," praised the action of the police and three of Roman Catholicism.

endeavoured to give its readers the reassuring impression that the strike was a total failure.

MORE THAN 50,000

African mine workers continue to join the strikers. The figures given by the capitalist press that 50,000 are on strike is underestimated. Many mines not mentioned in the "Star" and "Rand Daily Mail" press reports are out on strike. Sallies, Brakpan, Witpoort are all mines which were out on Tuesday morning.

Despite all efforts at intimidation, the spirit of the workers remains high.

Scores of workers and trade unionists assisting the union have been arrested on various charges.

SIX DEAD

AT SUB NIGEL MINE ON TUESDAY MORNING THE POLICE OPENED FIRE ON THE WORKERS. SIX WERE SHOT DEAD AND OTHERS WOUNDED. THE REPORT OF THE SHOOTING OF THE SIX WORKERS WAS GRAVELY DISTORTED BY THE CAPITALIST PRESS, WHICH TRIED TO MAKE OUT IT WAS THE WORKERS' FAULT.

U.S. SUPPORT FOR INDIANS

NEW YORK — A letter addressed to Hershel V. Johnson, U.S. delegate to UNO, Mr. Paul Robeson and Mr. Max Yergan, officers of the Council on African Affairs, asked for "maximum support" to the Indian Government's protest against discriminatory treatment of Indians in the Union of South Africa.

The letter states the position "brings into the foreground of international affairs the extraordinary and shameful practice of racial discrimination and exploitation practised by the Government of the Union of South Africa. For that reason the action of the Indian Government merits the approbation and support of all those who subscribe to democratic principles."

General Franco's Freedom

MADRID — What General Franco understands by religious freedom is quite different from what is understood by English-speaking peoples, as also by others. The "Bill of Rights" (Fuero de los Españoles) provides for "freedom of religious belief," but bars all religious rites and ceremonies except those of Roman Catholicism.

DEMOCRACY IN INDIA

NEW DELHI — For the first official admission has been that the total number of members of the Legislative Assembly in all provinces of British India is more than 1,610,692.

The violent reaction of the government showed Mandela one of the weaknesses of the white-dominated society. Because the bulk of the work force was black, the nation was vulnerable to united black protest. However, the great fear of the whites was that allowing blacks full voting rights would mean a black government that would expel "Europeans," as the white population was called.

Nelson tried to allay these fears in a policy document of the Youth League in 1948. He declared that "the cry 'Hurl the White man into the sea'... is extreme and ultra-revolutionary." He declared that the Congress Youth League professed a "moderate" stream of African nationalism. "We realize that the different racial groups have come to stay. But we insist that a condition of interracial peace and progress is the abandonment of white domination, and such a change in the basic structure of South African society that... exploitation and human misery will disappear. Therefore our goal is the winning of national freedom for African people, and the inauguration of a people's free society where racial oppression and persecution will be outlawed."

In other parts of Africa, black African independence movements began after World War II. In some countries, these movements were violent; in others, their leaders won independence through negotiation. However, all were destined to succeed. Today, only in South Africa do a minority of whites rule a black majority population.

In fact, the conditions of blacks were actually to worsen in South Africa. The clock was turned back further when the Afrikaner Nationalist Party (ANP) came to power in 1948. Previous white governments had been moderate by comparison. Under the leadership of Daniel Malan, this

South African newspaper,
August 15, 1946

party was committed to the policy of *apartheid,* "apartness of the races." The ultimate goal of apartheid was the complete separation of the races into areas where each group could "develop along its own lines." The word became a worldwide synonym for racism and injustice.

The Afrikaner government passed legislation that strengthened and systematized the discriminatory laws. In 1950, the Group Areas Act classified the country's population into four major categories: Europeans, Asians, Coloreds, and Bantus (Africans). It created a population register to fix the racial category of every person in the country. The towns and rural areas were divided into zones in which only one race could live, own property, and conduct business. Not surprisingly, the most desirable areas were set aside for whites.

The government closed the mission schools that had formerly educated blacks and Coloreds, and all nonwhites were excluded from the established universities. The government now took over the responsibility of educating blacks; it passed the Bantu Education Act of 1953. This act did away with most academic subjects and prescribed training in such activities as tree planting. Schooling was reduced to three hours a day.

Local laws created segregation in all areas where it formerly did not apply. Segregation was extended to buses, trains, movie theaters, and post offices.

Though it was necessary to admit nonwhites into the cities to work as servants and in industry, areas for their living quarters were set aside in "townships." The law now required women to carry passes.

Blacks not needed for labor were relegated to "homelands," based on the boundary lines of the old reserves. These homelands occupied 13 percent of the total area of the country, even though black Africans now made up 70 percent of the population. Typically, a man who held a job in a city was not able to get permission for his wife and children to live in the township with him. They had to remain in a distant "homeland."

One of the signs of apartheid,
at a beach in Durban

All forms of protest against the government were limited by the passage of the Suppression of Communism Act
of 1950. Under the guise of fighting communism, the government made illegal virtually any form of written or spoken opposition to government. Newspapers were censored,
books were banned, and many political meetings were outlawed.

Primary-school lessons in Transvaal, 1982

Squatters near Cape Town. Men must have permits to work in white areas, but when they move closer to their jobs they are not allowed to have their families live with them. The families move closer anyway, and camps like these are the result.

Mandela and his friends were naturally alarmed by the repressive new laws. The leaders of the Youth League confronted the leadership of the ANC and demanded a greater voice in the organization. Walter Sisulu was appointed secretary-general, and Nelson became a member of the national executive board.

Nelson and his allies adopted a more militant program for the organization. In a Program of Action policy issued in 1949, the ANC declared its intention "to employ the following weapons: immediate and active boycott, strike, civil disobedience, non-cooperation and such other means as may bring about the accomplishment and realization of our aspirations." In particular, they called for a one-day national work stoppage "as a mark of protest against the reactionary policy of the Government."

Nelson in particular advocated working harder to organize the mass of the black people. In what became known as the M plan (M for Mandela), he proposed organizing on a block-by-block basis in the townships. This would enable the ANC to build greater mass support, and it would involve greater numbers in the organization.

Despite Nelson's misgivings, the ANC also joined forces with the South African Communist Party and the Indian National Congress in calling for a national demonstration on June 26, 1950. The project met with only partial success. There was a complete work stoppage in Durban and several other small cities. Partial work stoppages took place in Johannesburg and Cape Town. However, the field workers in the Transvaal, which had been the responsibility of the ANC, failed to respond in great numbers.

Nevertheless, the 1950 demonstration forged an alliance between the ANC and the better-funded and better-organized Indian National Congress. In the years immediately afterward, Nelson became more interested in the techniques of passive resistance that Gandhi had used.

At the same time, he finished his law studies, and he and Oliver Tambo set up a law office in Johannesburg.

They rented space from a sympathetic Indian merchant. Most of their clients were victims of the apartheid laws. As Tambo recalled, "South African apartheid laws turn innumerable innocent people into 'criminals'... if, when we started our law partnership, we had not been rebels against apartheid, our experiences in our offices would have remedied the deficiency.... Every case in court, every visit to the prison to interview clients, reminded us of the humiliation and suffering burning into our people."

In December 1951, the ANC's annual meeting approved the beginning of mass protests on April 6 of the following year. That date would be celebrated by white Africans as the three hundredth anniversary of the founding of the Cape Colony. The ANC decided to show the injustice of the apartheid laws by issuing a call for nation-wide defiance of them.

Nelson was placed in charge of the Defiance Campaign of 1952. Risking arrest, he traveled throughout the country, visiting houses at night to explain the plan to groups of people. The Indian Congress joined the effort, and Mandela declared to a crowd of Indians and Africans in Durban: "We can now say unity between the non-European people in this country has become a living reality."

Throughout 1952, groups of people banded together to defy the apartheid laws in whatever way they could. Some marched through "Europeans Only" entrances to train stations or post offices. Others stayed out after curfew or refused to carry their passes. Indians entered black townships. The police hauled thousands of people to jail.

Mandela had warned people not to retaliate, no matter what the provocation. His turn came in Johannesburg, when he addressed a meeting after the curfew time of 11:00 P.M.. He was arrested, along with many of those present, and cheerfully entered the police van. He remembered the brutality of the police, who shoved a prisoner down a flight of stairs in the police station, breaking his ankle. They

Yusuf Dadoo, president of the Transvaal India Congress, addressing a meeting outside the Johannesburg City Hall during the Defiance Campaign. Nelson Mandela is standing to the left of Dadoo.

refused Mandela's demand that the man be given medical attention, and Mandela spent a night listening to him groaning with pain.

Only around 8,500 people had actually broken laws, but the influence of the Defiance Campaign was greater than the number of people who participated. Many thousands of blacks became aware that it was possible to resist apartheid. Membership in the ANC soared. In repressing the campaign, the government had aroused the sympathy even of whites to the cause. At the trial of the campaign's leaders in November, the judge noted they had advised others to maintain "a peaceful course of action." He gave them suspended sentences on condition they did not repeat the crime.

In December, Nelson was elected deputy to Albert Luthuli, the new president-general of the ANC. The government issued "banning orders" against both of them, along with hundreds of other leaders of the ANC, the Indian Congress, and the labor unions. "Banning" was one of the chief weapons the South African government used against nonwhites who opposed its policies. These bans could be issued for any reason. Those who were banned could not move out of a prescribed area, attend meetings, or meet with more than one other person at a time. Mandela's ban required him to remain in Johannesburg for six months.

In the next few years, Nelson carried on his law practice with Oliver Tambo. Because of his leadership of the Defiance Campaign, the Transvaal Law Society tried to have him disbarred, but the Supreme Court ruled in his favor. Mandela recalled, "In the courts we were treated courteously by many officials, but we were very often discriminated against by some and treated with resentment and hostility by others. We were constantly aware that no matter how well, how correctly, how adequately we pursued our career of law, we could not become a prosecutor, or a magistrate, or a judge."

The national government attempted to cripple the ANC

by banning its leaders from attending meetings. When new leaders were elected, they, too, were banned. The government would allow no opposition to its policies, nor would it permit the existence of any organization that attempted to challenge it.

In 1955, a call went out for a meeting of all progressive organizations to "draw up a Freedom Charter for a democratic South Africa of the future." The meeting was organized by a former teacher at Fort Hare College, Dr. Z. K. Matthews. In June, in a field at Kliptown, a number of organizations joined forces in response to that call. Among them were the ANC, the Indian Congress, the South African Congress of Trade Unions, and groups representing both Coloreds and whites.

The delegates cheered the reading of the Freedom Charter, which began, "We the people of South Africa declare for all our country and the world to know: that South Africa belongs to all who live in it, black and white, and that no government can justly claim authority unless it is based on the will of all the people." It urged a "one man, one vote" policy as the only means of attaining this goal. The Freedom Charter also called for an equitable sharing of the wealth of South Africa.

Nelson had been banned from attending the meeting, but he sent a message that was read to the crowd. He wrote an article that was published the following year calling the adoption of the charter "an event of major significance in the life of this country.... For the first time... the democratic forces irrespective of race, ideological conviction, party affiliation or religious belief have renounced and discarded racialism in all its ramifications, clearly defined their aims and objects, and united in a common program of action."

However, the issuing of the charter led to greater repression. The police conducted thousands of raids on the homes and offices of those suspected of supporting the charter. Nelson's papers were seized.

On December 5, 1956, Nelson was arrested along with

over a hundred other men and women throughout the country. Charged with violation of the Suppression of Communism Act, they defended themselves for the next six years in what became known as the Treason Trial. Nelson, who was often out on bail, helped to prepare the defense.

The strain of all these activities took its toll on his marriage. Nelson and his wife had three children, but the family was often separated because of Nelson's work with the ANC. He and Evelyn eventually were divorced.

During the Treason Trial, Nelson met Winnie Madi-kizela. Their meeting was to lead to marriage and a political partnership that would have a long-term effect on South Africa.

CHAPTER
3
WINNIE'S YOUTH

Nomzamo Winnie Madikizela was born in 1936 in the Pondoland region of the Transkei. Nomzamo—"she who strives," in Xhosa—was to be an appropriate name. The name "Winnie" was added at her baptism as a Methodist. She was the daughter of Columbus and Gertrude Madikizela. In this region most of the people were surnamed Madikizela. And Winnie, one of nine children, grew up in an extended family that often included twenty or thirty children whom Columbus had taken in.

Columbus was a history teacher in a government school. It was from him that Winnie learned of the history of her people. Columbus would give the textbook version of Xhosa history. Then he would say, "Now, this is what the book says, but the truth is: these white people invaded our country and stole the land from our grandfathers." In those days, before the Bantu Education Act of 1953, there was no difference between white and black education. Winnie was taught the traditional subjects, and she was an apt pupil. Columbus watched with pride as Winnie, at the age of eight, faced the Afrikaner examiners and gave totally correct answers.

Columbus was admired by his neighbors. But the family's life was hard. A teacher's salary did not go far with nine children to support. Winnie recalled, "I became aware at an early stage that the whites felt superior to us. And I could see how shabby my father looked in comparison to the white teachers. That hurts your pride when you are a child; you tell yourself: 'If they failed in those nine Xhosa wars, I am one of them, and I will start from where those Xhosas left off and get my land back.'"

Winnie's mother, Gertrude, was also a teacher. According to Winnie, her mother was a religious fanatic: "When I was only eight years old we used to get locked up in a room with her and my little sister, and she forced us to pray aloud. When my father was there, she would take us—two or three times a day—to a corner in the garden. It had high grass and formed some kind of protective shelter, and she would pray. We had to follow her in these religious rituals, which we didn't understand."

Gertrude was devastated by the death of one of Winnie's sisters from tuberculosis. She evidently never recovered from the shock, and died from an illness soon after. Winnie remembered later, "I watched her wither away, sitting in the dark corners of the house and praying silently. I think she could have had cancer. She lay there, just diminishing daily; for me as a little girl, she was literally disappearing, and she was in great pain; that's all I remember."

After her mother's death, Winnie had to leave school for half a year. She helped to take care of the other children. She also had to work in the fields, milk the cows, and tend the sheep and goat. When harvest time came, she had to gather in the "mealies," the staple food of the area.

Winnie showed early the spunk and intelligence which she never lost. She soon went back to school in a neighboring village. While in the nearby town, she saw a black family being attacked by a white youth over a trifling disagreement. No one came to their aid. The white store-

owners laughed, and Winnie's own father made no effort to interfere in the incident. That was the way life was in South Africa: blacks could not even defend themselves against whites.

Years later, Winnie remembered the feelings of rage and helplessness this event caused within her. She summed up the experience of growing up black in South Africa: "There is an anger that wakes up in you when you are a child, and it builds up and determines the political consciousness of the black man."

Winnie then went as a boarder to Shawbury High School, a Methodist school. Shawbury was an important experience for Winnie. She studied hard and did well academically. Socially she was well liked by her peers, and she began to show the leadership qualities that became more apparent later. In her senior year she was elected head prefect.

A school friend from Shawbury remembered Winnie: "She was elected chief-prefect for the supervision of all the girls from forms one to five. At that time she was very reserved and introverted but her leadership was to be seen early. We had these debating clubs and the way she disciplined the students and kept them together was remarkable. She had very good marks and she loved sports; she was very good at netball. She used to win trophies at the sports festivals at Umtata."

Winnie's years at Shawbury, the early 1950s, coincided with the time of ferment within the country. Many of her teachers were graduates of Fort Hare College. They were imbued with nationalist fervor in these days of the Defiance Campaign. It was here that Winnie first heard about Nelson Mandela.

Some of the students decided to strike to show their support with the protesters. Many refused to take their

Winnie Mandela in 1986

45

examinations. Winnie, who was conscious of the sacrifices that her father and sister had made to send her to school, maintained a low profile. The newspapers made much of the strike at the school. It came as a shock to some that young children would involve themselves in political issues. Many of the leaders of the strike were expelled from the school.

In later years, Winnie recalled their fate. She had been wise not to take part in the strike; if she had, she would not have been allowed to complete her education. Just one year after her graduation from high school, the government passed the Bantu Education Act of 1953. The government proclaimed, "There is no place for the Bantu in the European community above the level of certain forms of labor.... Natives will be taught from childhood that equality with Europeans is not for them. People who believe in equality are not desirable teachers for Natives." In future years, it would be impossible for an African to get an education like the one Winnie had. There were to be no more black lawyers or black doctors or black teachers. Africans were to be educated only to take their place within the country as menial workers.

After taking her examinations, Winnie returned home. She discovered that her father had remarried. His second wife was also a teacher. Hilda Nophikela was a sympathetic woman with whom Winnie soon established a warm relationship. Their close friendship was to be important to Winnie, and it continues to the present.

Winnie now had to decide what career she wanted to pursue. She was accepted at the Jan Hofmeyr School of Social Work in Johannesburg. This was a wonderful chance for Winnie, because the school was the only social-work school for blacks in South Africa. Part of her excitement about the acceptance arose from the opportunity to see Johannesburg. Winnie had never been out of the Transkei before and had never seen a large city.

When Winnie arrived at Johannesburg, she was greeted by the heads of the school, who helped her settle into her dormitory. Soon she was immersed in her work, and she knew that she had found her vocation. Social work gave Winnie the opportunity to serve others, which she craved.

At the Hofmeyr school, all the students seemed to be supporters of the ANC. But Winnie remained cautious about getting involved. The school officials had promised her father that if her grades were good, she would receive a scholarship. Winnie needed no further incentive and soon earned scholarship status. She rapidly became the top student at the school.

Nevertheless, she was becoming more politically conscious. She remembered later how thrilled she was to hear about the Freedom Charter. Though the government made it a crime to print or distribute copies of it, a few were passed from hand to hand. Winnie eagerly devoured its words. "It is my Bible," she says today.

Before she could complete her courses, Winnie was required to make a field study of a rural area. For this project, she chose the area in the Transkei in which Nelson Mandela had grown up. Though Winnie had already decided to dedicate her life to service, she was depressed by the conditions she found there. Although she herself had grown up in a Transkei rural area, she had never seen this kind of poverty. Malnutrition was common, and she watched helplessly while children died for lack of proper food and medical care.

In the midst of her study of the area, Winnie received some unsettling news. An old woman asked if she was pleased about the marriage. When Winnie asked whose marriage it was, she was told it was her own. Her father had arranged for her to marry the son of a local chief.

Winnie was shocked. Of course her father meant to tell her himself, but the real problem was that she did not want to be married to a stranger, not even the son of a chief. In a rural area, it was a wife's duty to do whatever her husband wished, and even though she might be of service among the people here, Winnie wanted more education.

Yet it was equally her duty to obey her father. The cultural tradition was a strong one, but finally Winnie decided to defy it, just as Nelson had several years earlier. She fled back to Johannesburg. There, she wrote her father a letter of apology, explaining her reasons for not wishing to marry. She added the news that she had been awarded a prize as the best student in the school, hoping this would ease his disappointment.

Winnie received her diploma with honors. Her achievement was particularly satisfying because she was the first student from Pondoland to attend the Jan Hofmeyr School. She was, however, to be one of the last. Soon after she left, the government closed the school under the Bantu Education Act. Henceforth, any higher education offered to Africans would be in "bush colleges" in the homelands.

Soon she was faced with another decision. She had been awarded a scholarship to continue her studies in sociology at a college in the United States. Naturally, she was overjoyed. She knew little of the United States, but allowed herself to fantasize about the life she might lead there. With time, she could prepare herself to return to South Africa and truly help her people.

A few days later, however, she received a letter from Baragwanath Hospital. It lay on the edge of the township of Soweto (short for the Southwest Townships outside Johannesburg) and was the only hospital in the area that would admit blacks. White patients were also treated there. Winnie had visited and lectured at the hospital, and the officials were impressed enough to offer her a job. If she accepted, she would be the first black medical social worker in South Africa.

For days, Winnie agonized over the decision. Her friends were delighted for her, whichever offer she chose. Her teachers and the head of the school told her it was her choice to make. Finally, she wrote her father, and he, too, said only she could decide. But his letter seemed to remind her that her country came first. It was what Winnie wanted to hear, and she accepted the post at the hospital.

At Baragwanath, one of those she worked most closely with was Dr. Nthato Motlana, an active member of the Youth League of the ANC. Like Nelson Mandela, he had been "banned" for his work during the Defiance Campaign.

Dr. Motlana remembered that working with Winnie "was most stimulating and encouraging. She was an outgoing personality, laughing a great deal, very cheerful and intensely concerned about other people's welfare. In hospitals you often find...staff...who are so impersonal, but Winnie was just the opposite."

Winnie did not let her duties end after hospital hours were over. She followed up mothers with newborn infants, visiting their homes in the areas. It gave her a chance to see the scope of the miserable conditions in black Soweto. Many of the houses were merely shacks made of iron sheets and cardboard. Scraps of rags and newspapers plugged up the cracks. Few of the young mothers knew about proper nutrition, and even if they did, their poverty was so great that they could not afford enough food for themselves and their children. The illegitimacy rate was high because of the government policy of separating families. Some mothers were so poor that they abandoned their babies.

Winnie enlisted the help of anyone who would lend a sympathetic ear. A reporter on a black newspaper helped her find the mothers of abandoned babies and raise funds to help others. She also became friends with some of the women at the hostel where she lived. One of her co-workers in the hospital was Adelaide Tsukudu, who was dating Oliver Tambo. When Winnie met Oliver, he recognized her name and announced that they were related. It was through Oliver and Adelaide that Winnie was to meet Nelson Mandela.

CHAPTER

4

THE TREASON TRIAL

Nelson Mandela, Oliver Tambo, and Walter Sisulu were only a few of the people who heard the police knock at their door on the night of December 5, 1956. All over the country, police rounded up Africans, Indians, Coloreds, and whites. In all, 156 persons were arrested and flown in government military helicopters to the Fort, as the prison in Johannesburg was known. The police broke into many homes and offices and searched them. The government announced that it had uncovered "a dangerous plot."

The arrests were the government's reaction to the meeting at Kliptown and the issuance of the Freedom Charter. The government charged the defendants with high treason. They were accused of being part of a conspiracy inspired by communism to overthrow the South African government by force.

The subsequent Treason Trial, which lasted for six years, ironically gave a lift to the African National Congress. It showed that the resistance movement was multiracial and widely based. Soon after the arrests, a Stand By Our Leaders movement was organized. Many prominent whites stepped forward to donate funds for the defense of the accused. The trial attracted the attention of the world press to the South African struggle for equal rights.

On December 19, 1956, the preparatory examination of the Treason Trial opened. From the early hours of the morning, crowds gathered in the streets around the courthouse carrying signs reading: "We Stand By Our Leaders." They sang the anthem of the Congress and other ballads of freedom. The following day the crowds were even larger, and police fired into the throngs to drive them away. Twenty-two people were wounded.

The prosecution narrowed in on the policy of the ANC from 1952 to 1956. The Freedom Charter was regarded as the crucial piece of evidence. The prosecution also accused the ANC of violence during the Defiance Campaign of 1952. Thousands of documents, including Nelson's speeches and published articles, were introduced as evidence. Among the documents were two signs that had been placed over foodstalls in the field where the Freedom Charter was first read to a crowd. The signs read, "Soup with Meat" and "Soup without Meat."

During this first stage of the trial, Albert Luthuli called for all citizens to stay at home for one day to protest apartheid and to demonstrate the need for a living wage. As Mandela explained, the call for citizens merely to stay at home, rather than invite violence by picketing, was to show the nonviolent character of the movement. The "stay at home" was particularly successful in Johannesburg and Port Elizabeth.

The preliminary stage lasted until September, when the court decided that it had enough evidence to hold a trial. Until the start of the trial, the defendants were free on bail to go to their homes. During this recess, the charges of high treason were withdrawn from Luthuli, Oliver Tambo, and many other defendants. But Nelson was not one of them.

Some time after Nelson's arrest, he met Winnie Madikizela. She had gone with Oliver Tambo and Adelaide Tsukudu, who had announced their engagement, to a small delicatessen. On seeing Nelson there, Oliver called him over and teased Winnie by asking if Nelson recognized her. Her picture had appeared in magazines when she took the job at Baragwanath Hospital.

Winnie says she remembers little about the meeting, because she was so nervous. Nelson, of course, was already a famous figure. He was thirty-eight years old, self-assured, and impressive to all who saw him. A white resident of Cape Town remembers seeing him striding along the street. Most black people tried not to attract attention when they were in white areas of the cities, but Nelson was different: "I noticed people were turning and staring at the opposite pavement and I saw this magnificent figure of a man, immaculately dressed. Not just blacks but whites...were turning to admire him."

Their first meeting was casual, but Nelson did not forget Winnie. During the trial, he called her at Baragwanath Hospital and asked her to lunch. He took her to an Indian restaurant where he watched amused as she tried to eat curry, a new experience for her. Winnie noticed that in any public place, they could never be alone. People were drawn to Nelson. "As we were eating, he couldn't swallow one spoonful without people coming to consult him."

The next day Nelson called again, and soon Winnie was seeing him on a regular basis. Even at this time, she explains, "Life with him was a life without him. He did not even pretend that I would have a special claim to his time." Winnie also noted that Nelson "was a fanatic from the fitness point of view." He often sent friends to pick her up at the hospital and bring her to the gym where he was working out.

She became a part of his circle of friends and thus was drawn into the political action. Each night he would meet with his personal friends between political consultations in the townships.

One day Nelson startled Winnie by saying: "You know, there is a woman, a dressmaker; you must go and see her. She is going to make your wedding gown. How many bridesmaids would you like to have?" It was a strange proposal, but Winnie understood. There was never any time for "frivolous romance." In response to his "proposal," she merely said, "What time?"

Nelson did speak with her seriously about what marriage would mean. He warned her that life with him would have drawbacks. He was on trial, constantly hounded by the police even while on bail. If she married him, she would be subject to the same kind of harassment. In addition, he had dedicated his life to obtaining freedom for his people, and this would take precedence over personal feelings. "It is a commitment for life," he said, "like a call to the ministry."

Because Nelson was under a banning order, he could not travel to talk to Winnie's father. So Winnie returned to Pondoland to tell Columbus herself. His reaction was not entirely favorable. He was honored that Winnie had attracted such a prominent man. But at the same time he had misgivings. Nelson was a target of the government and on trial for treason. Also, he was a divorced man with three children. Columbus was amazed that Winnie had earlier turned down two men who might have made superior husbands. One of those who had asked to marry Winnie was Nelson's childhood friend and relative, Kaiser Matanzima. Winnie's stepmother interceded for her and persuaded Columbus that he should accept Winnie's choice.

Nelson sent his relative George Matanzima to negotiate the bride-price, or *lobola*, with Columbus. The *lobola* is traditionally paid in cattle, and the amount is kept secret from the bride. To this day, Winnie does not know what her *lobola* was.

Later, when Nelson's papers were seized, the government security forces took the letter her father had written to Nelson acknowledging payment of the *lobola*. Years later, when Winnie was being interrogated, the head of the

Nelson and Winnie Mandela
on their wedding day,
June 14, 1958

security forces sneered, "Poor Nelson, he must have been terribly stranded to pay so much for a woman like you."

Nelson, still under ban, was granted four days to attend his own wedding in June 1958. It was held in Pondoland at Winnie's home. Following the Methodist ceremony, the couple celebrated happily with a few relatives and friends. At the end of the four days, Nelson and Winnie headed back to Johannesburg. They had not had time to cut part of the wedding cake at the bridegroom's home, as was the custom. Winnie has kept it to this day, waiting for Nelson's release from prison.

They set up home in Orlando, a part of Soweto. Less than two months later, the Treason Trial began. All of the ninety-one remaining defendants pleaded not guilty. There were observers at the trial from all parts of the world. The trial made for great inconvenience for the Mandelas. It was held in Pretoria, so Nelson had to commute from Johannesburg each day. Also, Nelson sometimes slipped away to attend clandestine political meetings. As a result, there was little time for a traditional home life. It was at this time that Winnie joined the ANC and, to increase her effectiveness, took lessons in public speaking. In addition she had her social work to attend to.

Soon after their marriage, Nelson and Winnie were awakened in the middle of the night by a banging on their front door. It was the security police. Winnie recalled, "There were these coarse Boer policemen thumbing through our personal belongings, pulling books off shelves, rough handling our possessions and all the time passing derogatory and derisive remarks about *kaffirs* [a vulgar Afrikaans term for blacks, roughly equivalent to "nigger"]. It was horrible. And it was all for nothing. They couldn't find anything incriminating... Nelson warned me I would have to get used to raids like that, but afterwards they never seemed quite so traumatic as that first time...."

Further government harassment was directed against the law firm of Mandela and Tambo. They were ordered to leave their quarters in the Indian section of Johannesburg and practice in a township "at the back of beyond." Nelson remarked that the order "was tantamount to asking us to abandon our practice, to give up the legal service of our people for which we had spent many years training. No attorney worth his salt would agree easily to do so." Tambo, now free from the accusation of treason, kept up the practice, and Nelson assisted him whenever he had time away from the trial preparations.

Just four months after their marriage, a women's march was organized to protest the extension of the pass system to women. Winnie, as a member of the Women's League of the ANC, was in the forefront of the protesters. As the women gathered to begin the march, they were arrested. Their sentence was a month in prison.

Now pregnant, Winnie was revolted by the dirt and stench of the prison cells. Her only consolation came from Albertina, the wife of Albert Sisulu, who was a trained midwife. Albertina wrapped Winnie in her own overcoat to keep her warm on the cold prison floor.

After her release from prison, Winnie gave birth to a daughter, who was named by a chief, according to African custom. The chief named her Zenani, which means "What have you brought?" This was shortened to Zeni.

The government ordered Baragwanath Hospital to dismiss Winnie from her job. Soon, however, she found work with the local Child Welfare Society. She would hold that post for the next four years.

There had been tensions within the ANC for many years over the nonracial ideal of the Freedom Charter. Those who called themselves Africanists wanted to "go it alone," without help from nonblack groups. Other members of the ANC wanted to maintain their cooperation with other racial groups in South Africa.

Africanism had a strong appeal to the youth of the

ANC. In earlier days, Mandela had shared some of the same thoughts. But he came to feel that the ANC had to take account of "concrete realities." The white South Africans had come to stay, as had the Coloreds and the Asians. He continued to hold to the ideal expressed in the Freedom Charter, that all South Africans should have equal rights and that all racial oppression and persecution should be banished.

In 1959, the tensions came to a head. A militantly nationalistic group broke away from the ANC under the leadership of Robert Sobukwe. This group formed the rival Pan Africanist Congress (PAC). The PAC did not want any cooperation with other racial groups. They strongly supported the slogan, "Africa for the Africans."

In 1960, the Pan Africanist Congress planned a passive resistance campaign against the pass laws. On March 21, Robert Sobukwe and others walked barefoot to the Orlando Police Department and offered themselves for arrest after burning their passes. They were immediately jailed.

Thirty-five miles (56 km) away, in Sharpeville, a township outside the city of Vereeniging, a crowd gathered in peaceful protest. When the police arrived, they shot into the crowd, killing 69 people and wounding about 180. Many were shot in the back while trying to flee. Eight women and ten little children were among the casualties. A few days later, police shot more demonstrators in Langa, a township outside Cape Town.

The Sharpeville massacre brought a wave of international condemnation on the South African government. The United Nations Security Council approved a resolution blaming the South African government for the shootings. Prices fell drastically on the Johannesburg Stock Exchange in anticipation of international economic sanctions.

All differences between the ANC and the PAC were put aside as president Albert Luthuli called for a day of mourning. Fearing a new wave of government repression, the ANC leaders decided to send a representative abroad,

*Some of the victims of the massacre
on March 21, 1960, in Sharpeville, a township outside the city of Vereeniging*

where he could operate without the restraint of the South African police. Oliver Tambo was selected for the job. Ever since, he has operated as the head of the ANC outside South Africa. Today he is based in Lusaka, Zambia.

Protest demonstrations erupted throughout the country. Albert Luthuli publicly burned his pass, as did thousands of others. For a few days the pass laws were suspended by the government, but they were then reinstated.

On March 30, the government declared a state of emergency. A series of mass arrests began, but the protests and strikes went on. On April 8, after declaring that the ANC and PAC were a "serious threat to the safety of the public," the government outlawed the organizations. Most of their leaders were arrested. The last act of the ANC was to call for a convention to discuss a new organization for the South African government.

One of those arrested was Nelson Mandela. Another was Albert Luthuli, who on his release was awarded the Nobel Peace Prize. On his return from accepting the prize, he was banished to a remote part of the country. Later, according to the government, he was killed by a train while walking along the track.

Other disturbances erupted over a separate issue of racial policy. The government had adopted a plan to set up Bantustans, or homelands, in outlying areas as a way of disposing of blacks who were not needed to work in white areas. Eventually, these Bantustans were to become independent. The Transkei was one of these Bantustans.

This plan led to fighting in the Pondoland region between black supporters and opponents of the policy. Winnie's father was threatened during the disturbances by antigovernment protesters. The government sent in troops, who brutally quelled the fighting.

Later, after a Bantustan government was set up, Winnie's father accepted a post as an official in it. The leader of the "independent" Transkei Bantustan was Kaiser Matanzima; his brother George acted as his chief adviser. To the members of the ANC, any blacks who cooperated in the Bantustan relocation efforts were traitors. Because of her father's cooperation, Winnie became estranged from him.

The legal defense team in the Treason Trial had quit in protest against the state of emergency called by the government. Nelson, still in jail as a result of the roundup of ANC officials, began to conduct the defense himself. Hour after hour, day after day, he cross-examined witnesses and gave his own testimony.

All who watched his performance were affected by his dignity, his command of the facts, and his regard for the law. He frequently gave long, thoughtful answers in response to questioning by the judge and prosecuting attorneys. In one exchange, the prosecutor tried to show that Mandela knew that the actions of the ANC would bring about violence by the government. Mandela replied: "Yes, the Congress was of that view, my lords. We did expect force to be used ... but as far as we are concerned we took the precautions to ensure that the violence will not come from our side."

The judge also asked: "Well, as a matter of fact, isn't your freedom a direct threat to the Europeans?"

Mandela answered: "No, it is not a direct threat to the Europeans. We are not anti-white; we are against white supremacy and in struggling against white supremacy we have the support of some sections of the European population.... We said that the campaign we were about to launch was not directed against any racial group. It was ... directed against laws which we considered unjust."

After the state of emergency was lifted, Nelson went home each night, but the Mandelas' home life was, as usual, hardly a normal one. Winnie recalled, "There has never been a stage in my life where it was my husband and I and the children. He would come home from court and say, 'Darling, I brought my friends here to taste your lovely

*Celebration at the end of the Treason Trial,
when Nelson Mandela (at right) was acquitted*

cooking,' and he would pitch up with ten people and we would have one chop in the fridge."

Almost nightly, Nelson was called out to meetings. Winnie said, "We became such total colleagues and comrades in the struggle that there was no such thing as him reporting to me when he was going to his meetings." And when he came home and found Winnie gone, "he would know that I had gone to my own meetings. We never even asked, how was it, at the end of the day. It was part of the life of that house."

In December 1960, Nelson heard that one of his sons was ill in the Transkei. He secretly traveled there, and while he was gone, Winnie gave birth to a second daughter, Zindziswa, nicknamed Zindzi.

In March of the following year, the trial ended, and Winnie waited nervously in the gallery of the courtroom when the verdict was announced. It was possible that Nelson could be found guilty and given the death penalty. A lesser penalty was life imprisonment. She could hardly believe her ears as she heard the judge say that, in "findings of fact," the state had failed to prove a policy of violence. Although the ANC showed a "strong left-wing tendency," continued the judge, the state had not proved it was communist or that the Freedom Charter advocated a communist state. He looked at the assembled defendants: "You are found Not Guilty. You may go."

The friends and relatives of the defendants cheered wildly. They began to shout, "Nkosi Sikelel iAfrika," which means "God bless Africa."

CHAPTER
5

THE BLACK
PIMPERNEL

Two weeks before the end of the Treason Trial, the government had allowed the banning order on Nelson to expire. Possibly it was an oversight on the part of a government official who expected Nelson to be convicted in the trial. In any case, he was now not only free from legal charges, but for the first time in years allowed to go wherever he wanted within the country. Perhaps more important, he could appear in public at political gatherings.

Winnie remembers Nelson standing outside the door of their home, with a crowd of people gathering around to congratulate him. He asked her to pack a few things in a suitcase. She went inside the house, but by the time she returned with the suitcase, he had already left. Later a friend came to pick up the suitcase. The next day she read in the afternoon newspapers that he had gone to a rally in Pietermaritzburg to address the All-in African Conference.

"That was the last I saw of my husband as a family man," she later wrote. "There had been no chance to sit down and discuss his decision to commit himself totally. I think he found it too hard to tell me. With all that power and strength he exudes, he is so soft inside. I had just noticed that week that he was silent and thoughtful.... Before washing his shirt one day, I found a document in the pocket. He had paid rent for six months—that was very unusual. So I think he was trying to ease the pain, trying to think of ways in which I would be able to face life more easily without him. And then the car. It was not in order, and he suddenly had it repaired, and just left it parked in the garage. That was the day he went underground."

Nelson used his temporary freedom from banning to go underground, because he realized that the struggle for black rights was about to take a new turn. The South African government was preparing to cut its ties to the British Commonwealth and the restraints on its actions that Commonwealth membership carried. The government had proposed that the country declare itself a republic. All that remained for approval of this step was a referendum in which only whites could vote. Passage was nearly a certainty.

The All-in African Conference at which Nelson spoke had been called to discuss what was to be done in response. Fourteen hundred delegates gathered—a cross section of the political and cultural leaders of black South Africa.

The appearance of Nelson Mandela electrified the crowd. The conference demanded that a new constitution be drafted, setting up a government with no color bar. The conferees decided that if their demands were not met, they would call for a three-day "stay-at-home" to coincide with the establishment of the republic on May 31, 1961. Nelson was chosen to head the National Action Council to organize the stay-at-home.

The government response was predictable—a new round of arrests. Anticipating this, Mandela had gone underground with other leaders. Throughout April and

Newspaper dated March 30, 1961

ALL-IN CONFERENCE
CALLS FOR
ACTION

ass Demonstrations On Eve of Republic

NEW AGE

Vol. 7, No. 24. Registered at the G.P.O. as a Newspaper 6d

SOUTHERN EDITION   Thursday, March 30, 1961   5c

Photos by Joe Gqabi and Bala Govender
and story from M. P. Naicker

MARITZBURG.

ALL AFRICAN PEOPLE'S CONFERENCE HELD AT PIETERMARITZBURG AST SATURDAY WAS AN UNQUALIFIED SUCCESS.

ver 1,400 delegates attended and unanimously demanded . . .

* "that a National Convention of elected representatives of all adult men and women on an equal basis irrespective of race, colour, creed or other limitations be called not later than May 31, 1961."

onference also resolved:

at should the minority overnment ignore this de-nd of the representatives the united will of the rican people . . .

1. To call on the people to organise mass demonstra-tions throughout the coun-try on the eve of the decla-ration of the Republic on May 31.

2. To call on all Africans not to co-operate or colla-borate with the proposed S.A. Republic or any other form of Government which rests on force to perpetu-ate the tyranny of a mino-rity; and, to organise and unite in town and country to carry out constant ac-tions to oppose oppression and win freedom.

3. To call on the Indian and Coloured communities and all democratic Europeans to join forces with us in opposition to a regime which is bringing South Africa to disaster . . ."

The highlights of this magnificent Conference were . . .

● The patience and seriousness with which the delegates from all over South Africa met and discussed the problems that faced them. They conferred throughout Saturday night, even though many of them were tired after travelling the previous night in order to get to Conference . . .

● The inspiring opening address by Mr. Nelson Mandela, for-mer President of the banned African National Congress (Transvaal), whose every sen-tence was either cheered or greeted with cries of "shame" when he referred to atrocities perpetrated against the people by the Nationalist Govern-ment.

● The representative character of the delegates, old and young, who had travelled many miles to be at Confer-ence. There were delegates from Thogazi in Zululand; St. Faith's, near Port Shepstone; Ixopo, New Hanover, Tembu-land, Pondoland, Zeerust and Sekhukhuneland.

They came from New Brighton and Moroka, Alexandra and Langa,

(Continued on page 3)

Mr. Nelson Mandela delivering his inspiring opening address to Maritzburg conference.

AFRICA DAY SPECIAL

In commemoration of Africa Day (April 15), New Age will distribute FREE with each copy of the paper | published on Thursd April 13, a portrait Chief A. J. Lutuli. Order your copy now.

doning the first hall, which had been wired by the Special h, the people marched two miles in the rain to another hall n Plessislaer where the conference eventually took place.

TREASON TRIAL MA
END THIS WEEK

JOHANNESBURG

THERE WAS AN ELECTRIC ATMOSPHERE IN THE TREASON TRIAL COURT WHEN JUDGES ADJOURNED THE CASE LAST FRIDAY UNTIL WEDNESDAY OF THIS W IT LOOKED AS THOUGH AFTER FOUR AND A HALF YEARS OF PAINFUL NEVER-END EVIDENCE AND ARGUMENT THE BIG CASE MIGHT SUDDENLY COLLAPSE.

The judges broke into the Defence argument when Advocate A. Fischer was on his arguing on the meetings the 28 accused had addressed. The presiding judge, Mr. J Rumpff, said the Bench thought it might shorten the proceedings if it interrupted the De argument and adjourned for six days for the judges to consider the legal points so far ar

The Crown argument has lasted almost four months. The Defence has been argui three weeks. This is the second interruption of the Defence argument by the Bench. The was to call on the Crown to answer the weighty legal arguments advanced by the Defenc fore its case was fully argued. This second adjournment was called for by the Bench afte Trengove had already completed the Crown's reply to the Defence legal argument.

(Continued on page 6)

May, he toured the country secretly with Walter Sisulu. He found a welcome in many homes, even though the penalty for harboring a wanted fugitive was harsh. At night, he addressed groups assembled in secret to hear his call to action.

In a letter published in the press, Nelson explained that going underground was the only course of action left open to him: "I have had to separate myself from my dear wife and children, from my mother and sisters, to live as an outlaw in my own land. I have had to abandon my profession and live in poverty, as many of my people are doing. ... The struggle is my life. I will continue fighting for freedom until the end of my days."

He also sent letters to the head of the government, Hendrik Verwoerd, and to the leader of the main opposition party in the country's parliament. Mandela told Verwoerd, "We have no illusions about the counter-measures your government might take.... We are not deterred by threats of force and violence." To the opposition leader, he pleaded for support in the call for a constitutional convention. "It is still not too late," he wrote. "A call [from you] for a National Convention... could well be the turning-point in our country's history. It would isolate the Nationalist government and reveal for all time that it is a minority government." Neither letter drew a reply. The plans for the stay-at-home continued.

The government took strong measures to disrupt the plans. Its security police had developed a highly effective spy network, and they arrested some ten thousand people. Meetings were banned and printing presses seized. Mandela continued to elude capture, passing through police road blocks even though his tall, striking figure seemed to make him easily recognizable. He went from township to township, speaking and distributing leaflets.

The foreign press had gathered, expecting another Sharpeville. The London *Observer* described the climate of fear that had come over the country: "Scores of citizens' force and commando units were mobilized in the big towns.

Camps were established at strategic points; heavy army vehicles carrying equipment and supplies moved in a steady stream...helicopters hovered over African residential areas and trained searchlights on houses, yards, lands and unlit areas.... Police vans patrolled areas and broadcast statements that Africans who went on strike would be sacked and forced out of the town."

The whites clearly feared a violent reaction on the part of blacks, despite Nelson's continual promise that no violence was intended—only a passive strike. The white fear stemmed from the central problem of South African society: that nonwhites vastly outnumbered whites, even though through sheer force of arms the whites controlled the economy and the society.

When the first day of passive protest came at last, hundreds of thousands risked arrest and the loss of their jobs by participating. Even so, the stay-at-home was a disappointment. The government had done its job well. Mandela acknowledged this by calling the strike off on the second day. On being interviewed by a foreign correspondent in a secret location in Johannesburg, Mandela observed, "In the light of the steps taken by the government to suppress it, it was a tremendous success."

For the next year and a half, Nelson continued his work underground, avoiding arrest, surfacing only long enough for brief meetings before disappearing again. He was always in danger of being turned in by informers. He was the most wanted man in South Africa. In spite of narrow escapes, such as the occasion when he had to slide down a rope from a second-story window to escape from a house the police were entering, he eluded the police traps. Stories about his escapades, mixing fact and fancy, circulated throughout the black townships. His very freedom was a demonstration of the government's lack of support among the black population. He began to be known as the Black Pimpernel, after the fictional character the Scarlet Pimpernel, who always escaped from his enemies.

For Winnie, it was a time of fear and anticipation. Fear that she would receive the news that Nelson had been captured or killed, and anticipation of the infrequent occasions when he slipped back into Johannesburg. Of this time, she wrote, "I waited for that sacred knock at the window at the early hours of the morning. I never knew when."

Sometimes, at the beginning, Nelson would slip back to their home in the early hours of the morning. Later, when the police set up a twenty-four-hour watch on their home, Winnie would receive messages telling her to meet someone in a car at a certain place. The driver would take her for a distance, where they would meet another car, and she would jump into that one. "By the time I reached him I had gone through something like ten cars. . . . The people who arranged this were . . . mostly whites. I don't know to this day who they were. I would just find myself at the end of the journey in some white house; in most cases when we got there they were deserted." Nelson and Winnie never had more than a brief time together before he had to go on running.

"I had so little time to love him," Winnie wrote, "and that love has survived all these years of separation."

On one occasion, someone came to Winnie at work and told her to drive to a particular corner. "When I got there," she wrote, "a tall man in blue overalls and a chauffeur's white coat and peaked cap opened the door, ordered me to shift from the driver's seat and took over and drove. That was him. He had a lot of disguises and he looked so different that for a moment, when he walked towards the car, I didn't recognize him myself."

Nelson Mandela when
he was known
as the Black Pimpernel

The successful government crackdown on the stay-at-home had been a watershed for the ANC. It was clear that the government would not respond to any nonviolent protest. Albert Luthuli had summed up the futility of the ANC's peaceful efforts before his death in 1967. Though a winner of the Nobel Peace Prize, he wrote, "Who will deny that thirty years of my life have been spent knocking in vain, patiently, moderately, and modestly at a closed and barred door? What have been the fruits of moderation? The past thirty years have seen the greatest number of laws restricting our rights and progress, until today we have reached a stage where we have almost no rights at all."

Many blacks, especially the young, reached the same conclusion, without expressing it in such idealistic terms. There was talk about terrorist acts against whites. Many in the leadership of the ANC felt that something had to be done or the organization would lose the allegiance of the youth.

For the first time, Nelson himself began to show signs of losing faith in the methods of nonviolence. After the cancellation of the stay-at-home, he told a reporter, "If the government reaction is to crush by naked force our nonviolent struggle, we will have to reconsider our tactics. In my mind we are closing a chapter on this question of a non-violent policy."

With the blessing of the ANC leaders, Nelson was placed in charge of a group that would become known as Umkhonto we Sizwe, "the Spear of the Nation." This group was to operate outside the ANC to sabotage installations within the country. In the group's actions, an attempt would be made to ensure that no lives were lost. The targets were to be government installations and buildings. Its first action was carried out in December 1961. Electric installations, Bantu Affairs offices, and municipal offices were bombed in Johannesburg and Port Elizabeth. One of the saboteurs was killed in the explosions. Many Africans were thrilled by the actions.

At the time of the first action, Umkhonto issued a manifesto that stated, "We...have always sought...to achieve liberation without bloodshed and civil clash. We hope... that our first actions will awaken everyone to a realization of the disastrous situation to which the Nationalist policy is leading.... The time comes in the life of any nation when there remain only two choices: submit or fight. That time has now come to South Africa."

After the first action of Umkhonto, the government's search for Nelson intensified. Early in January 1962, he left the country. Oliver Tambo had arranged for him to speak at the Pan African Freedom Conference in Addis Ababa, Ethiopia. Merely by leaving South Africa, he added to the "crimes" he would be charged with.

At the conference, Nelson outlined the situation within South Africa and thanked the delegates for their nations' support in the attempt to boycott South African goods. About the actions of the Umkhonto, he said, "a government as strong and as aggressive as that of South Africa can never be induced to part with political power by bomb explosions in one night and in three cities only. But in a country where freedom fighters frequently pay with their very lives...planned acts of sabotage...are a demonstration of the people's unshakable determination to win freedom, whatever the cost may be."

After the conference Nelson and Tambo toured many countries in Africa. At all stops they met with support for their cause. Nelson was inspired by the fact that the growing nationalist movement was leading to independence in the other African nations. In Algeria, Nelson arranged for military training for Umkhonto recruits and toured military camps. After the African tour he went on to London, where he was received by British Labour Party leaders.

Nelson had never been outside South Africa before, and the experience was revealing. For the first time he was a free man: "Free from white oppression, from the idiocy of apartheid and racial arrogance, from police molestation, from humiliation and indignity. Wherever I went I was treated like a human being. In the African states I saw black and white mingling peacefully and happily in hotels, cinemas: trading in the same areas, using the same public transport, and living in the same residential areas."

Personally, he must have yearned to remain where he was, not only free, but idolized as the leader of the freedom struggle in South Africa. But he knew that he was becoming a symbol of hope to his people. He returned to South Africa as secretly as he had left.

Sabotage had continued during his absence. He reported on his trip and was brought up to date on the Umkhonto missions. He then traveled to Natal Province, where he met with Albert Luthuli. Luthuli was disturbed by the Umkhonto policy and upset that he had not been consulted. He was informed that the decision to exclude him and other leaders was to protect the ANC from involvement in the sabotage.

On his way back to Johannesburg, Mandela was stopped by three carloads of police who had been tipped off by an informer. Nelson's capture came on August 5, 1962, after he had evaded the police for seventeen months. He was imprisoned in the Johannesburg Fort.

Winnie recalled, "The way I got the news of his arrest was terrible. I was at work at the Child Welfare offices and I was on my way out....I bumped into one of his friends—the way this man looked! He was white like a ghost, his hair was standing on end.... I associated him so much with my husband that I found myself asking, 'Is he all right?'...And the reply was 'No, we think he'll be appearing in the Johannesburg court tomorrow.' Then of course I knew what that meant.... I knew at that time that this was the end of any kind of family life, as was the case

*Winnie Mandela with
the Mandelas' daughters,
Zindzi (left) and Zeni*

with millions of my people—I was no exception. Part of my soul went with him at that time."

On August 8, Mandela stood in court impassively as the charges were read. He was accused of inciting workers to strike in 1961 and leaving the country illegally. Then he was led away to a cell in handcuffs. Winnie watched from the public gallery.

On the walls of townships, the slogan "Free Mandela" was written. There was an international outcry. The International Commission of Jurists compared the South African justice system to the "most extreme dictatorships of the left or the right." The government tightened its laws further. It was made a crime for one banned person to speak to another. Husbands and wives who were banned had to apply for dispensation from the government to speak. Walter Sisulu and many others were placed under twenty-four-hour house arrest. All gatherings that supported Mandela were banned.

On October 22, 1962, Mandela's trial opened in Pretoria. A crowd had gathered, to which he called with raised fist, "*Amandla!*" (Power!), to which the answer came "*Ngawethu!*" (To the people!). Then Nelson addressed the judge, "I hope to be able to indicate that this case is a trial of the aspirations of the African people, and because of that I thought it proper to conduct my own defense." He went on to challenge the ability of the court to hear his case. "I consider myself neither legally nor morally bound to obey laws made by a parliament in which I have no representation. In a political trial such as this one, which involves a clash of the aspirations of the African people and those of whites, the country's courts, as presently constituted, cannot be impartial and fair."

As the trial went on, Mandela cross-examined government witnesses. He asked why his letter to the prime minister had not been answered. He suggested it was "scandalous" that the prime minister of a country would refuse to answer a letter written on behalf of the majority of the population.

He defended his role in calling for a convention to write a color-free constitution on the grounds that he was acting to prevent violence in the country. "The government has set out not to treat with us, not to heed us, not to talk to us, but rather to present us as wild, dangerous revolutionaries, intent on disorder and riot, incapable of being dealt with in any way save by mustering an overwhelming force against us."

Nelson was found guilty on both counts. At his sentencing hearing he addressed the court: "It has not been easy for me ... to separate myself from my wife and children ... to take up the life of a man hunted continually by the police ... but there comes a time, as it came in my life, when a man ... can only live the life of an outlaw because the government has so decreed to use the law to impose a state of outlawry upon him. I was driven to this situation and I do not regret having taken the decisions I did take." Afterward, he was sentenced to five years in prison.

Nelson was taken to the prison in Pretoria, where he spent his days sewing mail bags. Later he was transferred to Robben Island, a dreary penal colony outside Cape Town.

Nelson's imprisonment did not halt the campaign of sabotage. The government could only respond with more arrests. New, more draconian, laws were passed. The punishment merely for membership in an "unlawful organization" was changed from five years to the death penalty.

The security police were rounding up people right and left. They made their most spectacular arrest in July 1963. They found the safe house outside of Rivonia (near Johannesburg) that was the headquarters of the outlawed ANC. Mandela had stayed there at times when he was underground. Walter Sisulu and eight other men were captured, along with many documents.

Robben Island, South Africa's
maximum-security prison,
seven miles from Cape Town

When it was found that the documents mentioned Mandela's activities, he was added to the trial of the other men. Nelson was transferred from Robben Island to a prison in Johannesburg. The defense lawyers and his fellow prisoners were shocked at the sight of him. He had lost forty pounds, and the prison uniform of boy's shorts and shirt hung limply on him. His skin had a yellowish tinge. But still he kept his impressive way of carrying himself. Being with his political friends seemed to have a tonic effect on him. As the days went on, he became his old self again.

The defendants were charged with recruiting members for sabotage and the violent overthrow of the government. The death penalty was a possibility. They pleaded Not Guilty. It took the prosecution five months to present its case. Many documents relating the discussions of the African National Congress were submitted as evidence.

When it came time for the defense to present its case, Mandela led it. He described how he had organized Umkhonto and the reasons for doing so: "I do not...deny that I planned sabotage. I did not plan it in a spirit of recklessness, nor because I have any love of violence. I planned it as a result of a calm and sober assessment of the political situation that had arisen after many years of tyranny, exploitation, and oppression of my people by the Whites." Mandela specifically denied the involvement of Umkhonto in many of the 193 acts of sabotage cited in the prosecution case.

He went on to describe the history of the African National Congress's efforts to change the apartheid laws, even after the ANC was declared an illegal organization: "The African people were not part of the government and did not make the laws by which they were governed. We believed in the words of the Universal Declaration of Human Rights, that 'the will of the people shall be the basis of authority of the Government,' and for us to accept the banning was equivalent to accepting the silencing of the Africans for all time."

Mandela pointed out the violent government response, at Sharpeville and other places, to the ANC's attempts to use nonviolent means to change the system. According to Mandela, Umkhonto was established because, "after a long and anxious assessment of the South African situation, I and some colleagues came to the conclusion that as violence in this country was inevitable, it would be unrealistic and wrong for African leaders to continue preaching peace and non-violence at a time when the Government met our peaceful demands with force."

He took up the government accusation that the ANC was communist because it had accepted communist aid and that the ANC's aims were the same as those of the Communist Party: "The ANC, unlike the Communist Party, admitted Africans only as members. Its chief goal was, and is, for the African people to win unity and full political rights. The Communist Party's main aim, on the other hand, was to remove the capitalists and to replace them with a working-class government. The Communist Party sought to emphasize class distinctions whilst the ANC seeks to harmonize them. This is a vital distinction."

As for cooperation between the communists and the ANC, Mandela pointed out that they shared the goal of removal of white supremacy, but pointed out that in the fight against Hitler, the United States and Great Britain had cooperated with the Soviet Union. Even so, "Nobody but Hitler would have dared to suggest that such cooperation turned Churchill or Roosevelt into communists or communist tools, or that Britain and America were working to bring about a communist world."

After four hours of speaking, he left his notes and ended with the statement, "During my lifetime I have dedicated myself to this struggle of the African people. I have fought against white domination, and I have fought against black domination. I have cherished the ideal of a democratic and free society in which all persons live together in harmony and with equal opportunities. It is an ideal which I hope to live for and to achieve. But if needs be, it is an ideal for which I am prepared to die."

In the end, the court found Nelson and all but one of the other defendants guilty. The sentence would be issued on the following day. From dawn, a huge crowd gathered outside the Palace of Justice. They carried banners proclaiming, "We Are Proud of Our Leaders" and "No Tears: Our Future Is Bright." They were prepared for the worst, but the judge exercised "the only leniency which I can show" and sentenced the defendants to life imprisonment.

When Winnie came out on the courthouse steps, a reporter for the London Observer said, "I fully expected to see [her] shaken. But no. She appeared on the steps and she flashed a smile that dazzled. The effect was regal and almost triumphant, performed in the heart of the Afrikaner capital in her moment of anguish, and the crowds of Africans thronging Church Square, with Paul Kruger's statue in the middle, loved it. They cheered, perhaps the only time black people have ever summoned the courage to cheer in that place."

The crowd outside shouted again, "*Amandla! Ngawethu!*" as the prisoners were driven away. Winnie recalled trying to get close to the police van so that her daughters, four and five years old, could see their father one last time. But it was impossible to get through the crowd. Then "someone grasped my shoulder. I turned and what do I see? A huge policeman, a member of the Security Branch, and he says, 'Remember your permit! You must be back in Johannesburg by twelve o'clock!' Here I was with my people, singing the national anthem, and there is this man with his hand on my shoulder repeating that I must go back to Johannesburg! All I could do was kick him and ignore him. Can you imagine! The last day! My husband is sentenced to life and I must think in terms of permits and the time of day."

CHAPTER
6
WINNIE ALONE

However she appeared to others, inwardly Winnie was devastated. Faced with the prospect of spending the rest of her life without Nelson, she tried to throw herself into her work. Worse than anything else, she remembered, was the loneliness, which was "worse than fear—the most wretchedly painful illness that the body and the mind could be subjected to. When you suddenly realize that you are stripped of a man...of whom you were just a shadow, you find yourself absolutely naked. He was a pillar of strength to me. I fumbled along and tried to adjust. It was extremely difficult."

Nelson was permitted to send her one letter of five hundred words every six months. The first one she received helped to raise her spirits. She read it over and over until the second one came six months later.

In addition to the letters, she was allowed to visit her husband twice a year. The visits lasted for only a half-hour, and Nelson and Winnie were separated by a screen. A security policeman listened to make sure that there were no political references. They were only allowed to talk about family matters.

Even though it was difficult and expensive to get to Cape Town, Winnie looked forward eagerly to each visit. It was here and in her letters that she felt she was keeping her family together.

At their last meeting before he went to prison, Nelson had warned Winnie of the difficulties she would face. He had said she would have to deal with jealous people who would vilify her. In addition, because of her relationship to him, she would become the target of intense government harassment.

This was to be the case. Her natural inclination was to trust people. Yet two of her close friends turned out to be police informers. The security police made efforts to break her spirit. In 1965, her anti-apartheid activities brought another banning order on her, for five years' time. She was restricted to the township of Orlando in Soweto. This meant she could no longer carry on her work with the Child Welfare Society. She found out that the society had only been able to employ her by paying her salary out of its own funds rather than from the government subsidy that paid others.

For a period she went from job to job. The government put pressure on her employers to fire her. She worked in a shoe store, a dry cleaner's, a furniture shop—she lost all the jobs. One manager told her he had been informed by the police that she could keep her job if she divorced Nelson.

For Winnie, one of the most terrible things to endure was the hardship placed on her children. She had a difficult time placing them in a school. The government pressured the schools to expel them soon after they were accepted. Under the terms of her ban, Winnie was forbidden to enter any educational institution and so had to ask a relative to take the children to school. "When you are a mother, that first day in school for your child is one of the greatest things. It means so much both to you and your child. I've never been able to do that." Worse yet, she learned that anyone who registered her children at school was taken to the headquarters of the security police and interrogated.

Finally, Winnie sent Zeni and Zindzi to school in Swaziland, a small black state adjoining South Africa. It was hard to send her children away, but it was the only way for them to receive a decent education. And when her daughters came home on holiday, she gave them all the love she could.

In 1966, the government placed additional restrictions on Winnie. Declaring her an enemy of the state, it prohibited her from "preparing, compiling, publishing, printing or transmitting any document, book, pamphlet, record, poster, photograph, etc." The following year, the police broke into her home to make sure she wasn't violating these restrictions. A policeman walked into her bedroom. She was only half dressed: "He finds me standing in this humiliating position in the bedroom and he continues as if I'm just a piece of furniture! And then he puts his hand on my shoulder! I don't know how he landed on his neck. All I remember is grabbing him, and throwing him on the floor, which is what he deserved. I remember seeing his legs up in the air and him screaming, and the whole dressing-stand falling on him. That is how he broke his neck (he did recover). I didn't know half the army was outside. I was carried to the car by six of them—with one stocking on, one shoe; I went to prison like that!" But she was soon released.

Meanwhile Nelson was confined in the prison on Robben Island, a bleak place in the Atlantic Ocean off Cape Town. He was facing a life term, and was only forty-five years old. At first he and the other political prisoners were kept in the old part of the jail, which had stood since the early days of colonization. A 30-foot (9-meter) wall separated the political prisoners from the black criminals. They were guarded by men with German shepherd dogs.

Nelson's cell was about 7 feet (2 meters) square and was lit by a weak light. There was no bed, only a bedroll and two blankets. There was only a pail for body wastes. When the prisoners were permitted to bathe, they were forced to run naked to the washroom in the new part of the prison. Their regulation shorts and shirts were no protection against the winter cold. They had to rise before sunrise for breakfast.

Even in small things, distinctions between races were enforced. At breakfast, each racial group was served porridge made from a different kind of grain. The Indians and Coloreds got a spoonful of sugar and some bread. Africans received only a half-spoonful and no bread. The rest of their meals consisted of corn, soup, and black coffee. Occasionally vegetables and a small piece of meat were supplied.

The African prisoners spent virtually all their time in the solitary cells, and they were warned by the guards to be silent—no singing or praying aloud. Added to the isolation was the lack of anything to do. Their first struggle was for the right to be allowed to leave the cell for exercise, to be able to speak to one another, to obtain water in the cells, and to be given better food. They won a small victory when they were allowed out to crush rocks, but the penalty for speaking was the loss of three meals. Sometimes, however, they could briefly trade messages under the noise of the hammering.

In the summer, they were taken out to labor in the limestone quarry. Their chains were removed, and they had to cut limestone and load it on a truck. The lime pit was like an oven, with the sun's glare reflected by the limestone, so that the men were scorched from above and below. All day they had to labor. When they finished in the afternoon, they were white from the limestone dust and completely exhausted.

When Nelson was unwell and unable to lift the rocks, he was penalized. He was sentenced to six days in solitary confinement and a diet of water in which rice had been boiled. Nelson had said, "South Africa's prisons are intended to cripple us so that we should never again have

Prisoners breaking rocks on Robben Island

the strength and courage to pursue our ideals." Through sheer force of will, he fought to keep up his physical and mental strength. He set for himself a routine of physical exercise, and according to fellow prisoners maintained a cheerful facade.

In the 1970s, the protests of international organizations won the prisoners some concessions: more food, better blankets, and the right to talk to one another. Now they had hot water for washing and an outside volleyball court. Once a month they were permitted to play table tennis and chess, and to see a movie.

However, the prison authorities found a new way to punish Nelson. The political prisoners were permitted to have paper only for study purposes and to write the twice-yearly letters. Now, in one of the regular searches of his tiny cell, the guards claimed to have found "memoirs." Nelson demanded that the officials show the evidence, but they refused. As punishment, Nelson's study rights were . taken away for four years. He was not allowed to have any books or news from the outside, except for letters from Winnie.

The work in the dusty quarry had damaged Nelson's eyesight, and he began to develop more serious health problems: high blood pressure and back trouble. The government, realizing that for him to die in prison might bring new international condemnation and demonstrations within the country, offered him a chance to be released. However, the government demanded that he first recognize the "independence" of the Bantustans. Nelson refused, replying, "The policy of separate development is wholly unacceptable."

The most difficult situation for Nelson was when he heard in 1969 that Winnie had been imprisoned.

The government had continued to harass her with random searches and questionings of anyone she might speak to. Undeterred, Winnie continued her work, and the government decided to act. On May 12, 1969, Winnie was awakened by the police at 2:00 A.M. They searched the house, removing the two children, who were home on holiday, from their beds so they could look under the sheets. They confiscated all of Nelson's old clothes, his typewriter, and every book in the house. Finally, they told Winnie that she was being detained.

In South Africa, the law permits the state to detain a person indefinitely without trial. It is a tactic often used against those who have committed no provable crime. Winnie was refused permission to contact anyone—lawyer, minister, relatives, or friends. The police took her daughters to the house of a relative, and they were without news of her for eighteen months.

For nearly all that time, she was kept in solitary confinement. During the first five months, she had no contact with anyone outside the walls. The conditions within her cell were much the same as those Nelson and the others endured, but she had not had time to prepare herself for them. The worst thing for Winnie, always a scrupulously clean person, was the utter filth of the cell. The diet of porridge and coffee, with only an occasional scrap of unwashed and slimy spinach or a tough scrap of pork fat, took its toll on her. She began to develop a skin infection due to a lack of vitamins.

The light in the cell was kept on day and night. To keep her mind active, she unraveled one of the urine-stained blankets she had been given and carefully rewove it. Her desperation for the sight of something living caused her to search the cell for insects—an ant, a fly. "You cannot imagine the joy there was in seeing a living creature," she recalled.

After a time, the police began to interrogate her. She never knew what time of day it was or how long they questioned her. She fainted often, but her interrogators revived her with questions. The chief interrogator warned her not to die until she had given the information that he wanted.

They had a long list of all the people Winnie had met

with for years—Nelson's friends, a young woman with a baby who had stayed at her house because she had nowhere else to go, anyone she talked to. The authorities wanted her to implicate these friends in plots to overthrow the government. The guards let her know that some of her acquaintances had been arrested too, and would soon confess. She learned later that some of them had been physically tortured, although the government could not afford to do that to a prominent person like Winnie.

After two hundred days of this treatment, Winnie learned that Nelson's lawyers had finally obtained an order from the Supreme Court of South Africa easing her condition. For the first time, she was allowed to take a shower. The chief interrogator appeared and flung a Bible, which she had requested, into her cell. He shouted. "There, pray to your God to have you released from detention. But you will pray in Xhosa, not in English!'" She had irritated him by replying to his questions in English, not in his native language of Afrikaans.

At last, she was brought to trial. It proved to be an embarrassment for the government. Witness after witness told the judge that they had been tortured to force them to testify against Winnie. Her younger sister, Nonyaniso, said she had been interrogated so much she no longer could tell the difference between what she knew and what the police had told her to say.

The attorney general announced he was abandoning the case, and the judge pronounced Winnie and those on trial with her Not Guilty of all charges. Among the things Winnie had been charged with were receiving instructions from a prisoner (Nelson) and reviving the outlawed ANC.

Incredibly, just after the judge's decision, the police arrived in the courtroom with machine guns and re-arrested all the prisoners. The whole process began again. Finally, at a second trial in September 1970, a second judge acquitted them once more.

Temporarily free to travel, Winnie went to visit her father in the Transkei. He was a cabinet minister in what was to become the independent Bantustan of the Transkei. He confessed to her that he had cooperated with the government plans for the Bantustan because he felt it would help their people. Now he realized that she had been right. The government was taking thousands of black Africans from the city areas and sending them to the Bantustans. They were given no help or training of any kind. They were merely parked there to fend for themselves until a need for them to work in the factories or mines arose again.

The rift between father and daughter was healed. Winnie visited him again in 1973 shortly before he died. He asked his wife to dress him in his best suit to meet his daughter and granddaughters. Standing painfully, he said, "I want you to remember me like this." She memorialized him as a "wonderful...character, imbued with compassion for his own people so unjustly treated...determined that the younger people should right the wrongs."

After her return to Soweto in 1970, Winnie was once more arrested. This time, her "crime" came about when she was taking her daughters home on a rainy day. Seeing a friend with a car, she called out to him for a lift. It was a measure of how closely she was followed that she was immediately arrested. The friend, like Winnie, was under a ban, and it was illegal for one banned person to speak to another one.

The government managed to get her sentenced to a year in jail. At the sentencing, Zindzi was in the gallery and burst into tears. Winnie spoke to her sharply: "You will *never* cry in front of a white policeman again."

An appeal reduced her sentence to six months. Perhaps through embarrassment, the government did not reimpose her banning order when she was released. She was to be free of it for ten months after thirteen years of banning.

During the years without Nelson, Winnie grew both as a person and as a leader of the struggle for black rights. She says of herself: "In the early years I was just a carbon copy of Nelson. I was no individual. If I said something, it was 'Nelson's wife' who said so. When he was no longer in the picture (I so hate talking about myself!), the public began to say I wasn't just a carbon copy as such; I had ideas and views of my own. I had my own commitment and I wasn't just a political ornament."

It took a while for the new woman to emerge. At first, after Nelson went to prison, she tried to carry on in his footsteps. As the time went by, she became more confident in presenting herself as an independent person. Though she found it difficult to speak in public, she forced herself to try, and she eventually became a forceful spokesperson for the struggle for equal rights.

Winnie brought to the struggle her own experiences in social work, which gave her an independent view of the reality of the black experience in the townships of the country. She found that her experiences in prison had toughened her instead of breaking her spirit. She wrote, "I got more liberated in prison....I am not saying it is best to be in prison. But...it is a question of which prison is better, the prison outside or inside—the whole country is a prison for the black man—and when you are inside, you know why you are there and the people who put you there also know."

Throughout the 1960s, virtually all the ANC leaders had been imprisoned. Ironically, by destroying the organization of black unity, the government only guaranteed that a more extreme one would arise. In the late 1960s, as conditions worsened in the townships, a new black consciousness movement arose. It was similar in thought to the black power movement in the United States, and had particularly great appeal for the young people. One of its leaders was Steve Biko.

In no part of the country was the movement more popular than in Soweto. Soweto had grown over the years so that by the middle 1970s it was one of the biggest sub-Saharan African cities. A high proportion of the people

Soweto Township, 1982

living there were teenagers and children. The government announced its decision to build some decent housing there. As usual, this concession had a qualification: residents could own their little homes only if they accepted citizenship in their appropriate homeland. Knowing that this meant they could be evicted and deported at any time, most of the people refused.

Ironically, the wave of militancy and black nationalism that swept through South Africa in the 1970s was led by those young people who had received a Bantu education. They had learned only enough to realize they were being educated for subservience to the whites.

In the early 1970s, the government announced that instruction in some subjects would be in Afrikaans, the language of the Boers. To the blacks, the language was that of their hated oppressor; furthermore, by denying blacks knowledge of English, the government was attempting to further cut them off from the outside world. The combination of the quality of the schooling, the teaching in Afrikaans, and the growing militancy among youth led to an explosion.

Winnie was aware of the growing militancy of the youth in Soweto. She told the authorities of her concern for the new measures. Her role as a leader in Soweto meant that many parents came to her with their problems. They told her that children as young as eight were staying away from school to protest the new regulations. Winnie was also aware that many of the youths felt contempt for their parents, believing that they had not fought hard enough against the system.

The students soon were working secretly through the Soweto Students' Representative Council to organize a peaceful march to protest the use of Afrikaans in the schools. To give the lie to the government's charge that outside agitators were responsible for the protests, the students would wear school uniforms. The older students tried to exclude those of grade-school age from the march, but even the youngest wanted to be a part of things.

Dr. Nthato Motlana, who had been Winnie's boss at the hospital years before, was now a leader in Soweto. He gave an eyewitness account of what happened on June 16, 1976: "I saw a stream of schoolchildren marching past my house.... I followed them to see where they were going. ...They had just reached the Orlando West school when the police tried to stop them marching any further. The children kept on walking so the police released dogs. I did not see the pupils set upon the dogs but...later I saw a dead police dog that had been burnt. Then the police panicked and fired into the mass of children.... I will never forget the bravery of those children. They were carrying [trashcan] lids to protect themselves and deflect the bullets. ...The police had dogs and tear gas and batons, but they chose instead to use bullets against those unarmed kids. The saddest sight anyone can see is a dying child ripped by bullets."

The shootings signaled the loss of government control over the area. For weeks, violence continued. The police rounded up as many people as the jails would hold. Dr. Motlana saw a van of police firing at a group of six-year-olds playing by the road.

Winnie, hearing the news of the first shootings while she was at work, rushed back to try to calm the situation. But on seeing their children shot down, adults now joined in the violence. More than fifty government buildings, including schools, were burned, as were shops, post offices, houses, and passing vehicles.

The government put the number of dead at six hundred, although other estimates are that over one thousand died,

Soweto, June 16, 1976.
The student being carried was
shot to death by police.

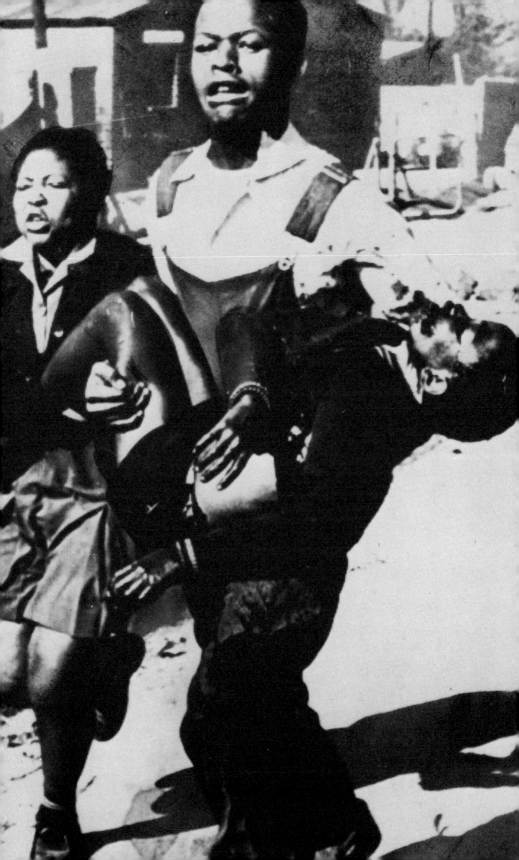

*Above: Alexandria, a township
adjoining exclusive white
suburbs of Johannesburg,
June 18, 1976
Opposite: Winnie Mandela
(right) at the funeral of Hector
Petersen, the first child to die
in the Soweto massacre*

and some four thousand were wounded. Most of the dead were children. Many of the protesters simply fled, and no one knows how many the police arrested. Winnie, Dr. Motlana, and other community leaders were arrested and held for months without charge or trial.

The world's press condemned the killing of the children. "Soweto" became a byword for cruelty and injustice, but the South African government ignored international protests.

CHAPTER

7

"WE ARE STRUGGLING FOR THE FREEDOM OF OUR PEOPLE"

Following Winnie's release from detention after the Soweto riots, she had four months of relative calm. Then, on May 16, 1977, with Zindzi home from school, she was awakened by the familiar knock at the door by the security police. On reaching for the packed suitcase that she kept ready for just such situations, Winnie was told to leave it. When she arrived at the police station, she became aware that something different was in store for her this time. Instead of being put in a cell, she was told to sit on a bench. In the cool night, she waited for hours before being informed that she would be banished to Brandfort.

Winnie had never heard of Brandfort. She was told that it was in the Orange Free State. While she was collecting herself, Zindzi arrived to tell her that the police had worked through the night clearing all her possessions out of her home for the trip to Brandfort. Zindzi had been offered the choice of staying in the empty house overnight and then returning to school, or accompanying her mother into exile. She chose exile.

Brandfort was located in the flat veldt of the Orange Free State. They drove through the town of Brandfort, a

cluster of neat little houses for whites only. Then they entered the black township in which children were playing in a huge garbage pit. Winnie was horrified to see children searching through the garbage for scraps of food.

Soon they reached a newly built square house that was to be Winnie's home. Convict laborers were still removing earth from inside the house. The house had no running water, no electricity, no covering on the earthen floors, and no sewage system. There was not even a shelf for kitchen utensils. Winnie's furnishings would not fit through the door. So the first night she moved some bedding into the house and fell asleep.

Winnie's Johannesburg employers continued to pay her salary for a whole year after her banishment. With this money, she bought herself the necessities. Brandfort had carried apartheid to extremes. Blacks were not allowed to enter the stores. Special windows were available where blacks could call out for items and then indicate when shown them whether they would buy.

To the amazement of the white clerks, Winnie just sailed through the front door and made her purchases. She and Zindzi even went to a clothing store and tried on some dresses. Winnie put on her most authoritative manner and carried the whole thing off. Before long, the other blacks in the area began to enter the stores, too.

Shortly before Winnie arrived, the local government gathered together the blacks of the area and told them that a dangerous woman would be coming to live among them. They warned the residents not to have anything to do with her. As a result, none of her neighbors greeted her when she first arrived. The government felt that Winnie would be further isolated by the fact that the local people spoke

Winnie and Zindzi shortly
after Winnie's banishment
to Brandfort

two African languages, Sotho and Tswana. Winnie knew neither of these languages. She spoke Xhosa and English. But Winnie set to work learning the local languages.

In spite of her own plight, she was touched by the human suffering that she saw here. Virtually every week there was a funeral for a black baby that had died because its mother could not afford to buy milk for it. Mothers tried to raise their children on a diet of flour paste and water, which only staved off malnutrition for a little while.

She observed that the black women of the area considered themselves lucky to find jobs as domestics in the white homes in the town. A "fringe benefit" was the meal of porridge and gravy or cooking oil that the whites gave their servants. The black women took most of it home to share with their families.

Nevertheless, she made some white friends. In this heart of Afrikaner country, most had never had social contact with a black. One of the women who faced the disapproval of her neighbors by befriending Winnie was Adele de Waal. She took Winnie books and let her use her tub for washing.

Soon after Winnie arrived in Brandfort, her older daughter Zeni got married. Her husband was one of the sons of the king of Swaziland. Winnie had to battle for permission to leave the country, but she succeeded in attending her daughter's traditional marriage ceremony.

Winnie's energy and commitment soon began to change things in Brandfort. She set an example by making her own home livable; she was soon organizing efforts to plant flowers in the township to make it more attractive. To remedy the terrible medical conditions that prevailed, she opened a clinic at her home. She used her own medical knowledge to treat minor ailments. In addition, she opened her home to women to teach handicrafts such as sewing and knitting. Even here, her activities were under constant scrutiny. A dour policeman named Sergeant Prinsloo was her shadow. He reported her for any minor infraction of the laws. Once, when she was visiting a neighbor, a man entered the house carrying a chicken. Winnie asked him how much it had cost. Sergeant Prinsloo burst in and arrested her for violating her banning orders by addressing a "gathering" of three people. In the local court, the prosecutor pointed out the dress she was wearing bore the colors of the ANC flag. Winnie received a suspended sentence for the offense, but the conviction was overturned on appeal.

The main reason for Winnie's banishment was that the government hoped to reduce her effectiveness as a national leader. She was well known by the members of the foreign press in South Africa, and the government had not been able to keep her from giving interviews. In addition, many blacks admired her courage and viewed her as a spokesperson for Nelson. Thus, she became a symbol of opposition to the government's policies. By sending her to this remote place, the police thought to prevent her from influencing public opinion. They were to find that it would not be so easy to silence her. Foreign newspaper reporters soon came to her little house in Brandfort.

It was illegal for any newspaper in South Africa even to quote the words of a banned person. However, Winnie used the international press to get her message across to the world. There was worldwide concern over her fate. Diplomats from many of the embassies in South Africa kept in touch with her. The German ambassador visited her and sent food for the township. He presented her with a television set so she could get news of the outside world. The only TV in the black township, it proved a source of fascination to the residents who crowded into her house. On such occasions, Winnie sat alone in another room, as at night she was not allowed to fraternize according to her banning order.

She did not feel as friendly toward U.S. diplomatic representatives. She told them not to call again, in protest against President Reagan's policy of "constructive engagement." This was the use of quiet diplomacy rather than economic sanctions or political condemnations to influence the South African government to abandon its apartheid policies. Winnie was not alone in believing that constructive engagement actually encourages the South African government to oppress blacks.

In addition, she has received many awards from societies in other countries. She was awarded an honorary doctor of laws degree from Haverford College near Philadelphia. She has never been allowed to leave the country to accept these honors, however. Her daughter Zeni and her friend Adelaide Tambo received the doctorate for her. Zeni also accepted the Freedom Prize awarded by two of Scandinavia's newspapers.

In January 1985, when U.S. Senator Edward Kennedy traveled to South Africa, he visited Winnie at Brandfort.

In July 1978, Nelson celebrated his sixtieth birthday. Although he remained on Robben Island, he was honored in the British House of Commons. People around the world sent thousands of greeting cards. Since he was not allowed to receive them, they were delivered to Winnie's address: No. 802, the Location, Brandfort.

Certainly the tribute dearest to his heart had to be a poem that was published that year by his younger daughter Zindzi:

> *A tree was chopped down*
> *and the fruit was scattered*
> *I cried*
> *because I had lost a family*
> *the trunk, my father*
> *the branches, his support*
> *so much*
> *the fruit, the wife and children*
> *who meant so much to him*
> *tasty*

Winnie and Senator Edward Kennedy
in Brandfort, January 9, 1985

loving as they should be
all on the ground
some out of his reach
in the ground
the roots, happiness
cut off from him.

The previous month, Nelson had been allowed the first contact visit since he went to prison in 1964. His elder daughter Zeni, as the wife of a Swaziland prince, had diplomatic privilege. This was Nelson's first human contact with his family since he had been imprisoned. Zeni, her husband, and their baby met Nelson in the visitors room. Zeni said, "He had never held a baby for sixteen years. He had seen us but never touched us. I thought he would break down. But I thought if I keep my strength, then Daddy won't [break down]. I went up to him, I nearly dropped the child...we must have held each other for a very long time. There were two policemen standing just behind my dad."

The letters that Winnie and Nelson have written to each other over the years became a source of solace to both. On one of the occasions when Sergeant Prinsloo hauled Winnie into court in Brandfort, Nelson wrote: "I will be thinking of you, especially as you are ordered to the dock....I am solidly behind you and know too well that you suffer because of your love of and loyalty to the children and me, as well as to our large family. It is an ever-growing love and loyalty."

Nelson wrote that without Winnie's letters and visits and her love, "I would have fallen apart many years ago." As part of his daily routine, he told her he dusted her photograph. "I start with that of Zeni, which is on the outer side, then Zindzi's and lastly yours."

Conditions within South Africa were not improving. After the Soweto riots, the government began a drive to capture the organizers of the youth movements. In 1977, Steve Biko, the leader of the black consciousness movement, died after being savagely beaten while under police custody. The South African government even sent commandos to attack the headquarters of the African National Congress in exile in Lesotho and Mozambique. In spite of all this, the government could not quell the opposition within its own borders.

Opposition remained strongest in the black townships outside the cities, particularly Soweto, and among the young children. Parents often found themselves ashamed in their children's presence because they knew the children believed that they were not militant enough. The twentieth anniversary of the Sharpeville massacre was celebrated with huge demonstrations.

In 1983, the government tried to divide the opposition by announcing that a new constitution would be written. Under it, there would be representation for the Colored and Asian population, but in separate parliaments. There would still be no national representation for the vast majority of the population who were black. In a referendum of white voters the constitution was adopted despite strong opposition from some ultranationalist groups that did not even want to allow these limited rights.

The new constitution was designed to appease the Coloreds and Asians and to split the movement advocating rights for all. However, it gave rise to a new, more widely based opposition group. The United Democratic Front (UDF) was formed in 1983 to oppose the new constitution. It included about four hundred separate organizations— black, white, Colored, and Asian—throughout the country. Trade unions, church groups, and student organizations all sent representatives to the first UDF conference. Winnie became a member, and Nelson managed to smuggle a message of solidarity out of the prison to be read to the delegates. Other supporters included the Colored leader Dr. Allan Boesak and black church leader Bishop Desmond Tutu, who was later to win the Nobel Prize for Peace.

The following year, elections were held for the new parliaments. Contrary to government expectations, the

turnout was low among the Asian and Colored population, particularly in the cities. Violence erupted during the campaign. The new parliaments were seen for what they were: window dressing. Their decisions could be overruled by the white parliament. Ironically, the move to create new parliaments caused a closer cooperation between the "beneficiary" groups and blacks.

It also gave rise to new leaders of the black opposition. Increased clashes with the police took place. The killing of blacks by the police produced huge funeral processions, and the cycle of violence continued. The nations of the world sent television crews to record the sight of policemen beating and killing blacks armed with stones. Blacks who were discovered to be police informers or collaborators were killed by other blacks. Even black leaders like Bishop Tutu were all but helpless to control the rage of their people.

The international protest that followed these television and newspaper reports caused the South African government to declare a state of emergency in 1985. Reporters and their cameras were no longer permitted in areas where disturbances occurred. All they could do was report the casualty statistics released by the government. South Africa became one of the few countries that could not afford to let the world see how it treated its people.

During his years in jail, the silenced prisoner on Robben Island became a symbol to the nation. The name of Nelson Mandela was on many protesters' lips. In the night, walls were covered with the message: "Mandela and Sisulu lead us." Although it was illegal even to quote Mandela in the country, and although many South Africans were too young

Black leader Steve Biko,
who was beaten to death
by police in 1977

*Above: Desmond Tutu, the archbishop of the
South African Anglican Church, photographed in
1985 when he was still a bishop. He is addressing
fifty thousand people who attended a funeral for
fifteen victims of unrest in Kwa Thema.*
*Right: Uitenhage, April 13, 1985. Mourners carry
twenty-seven coffins to burial grounds in a mass
funeral for victims of the police during the
twenty-fifth anniversary of the Sharpeville massacre.*

to have ever seen him, he assumed mythic proportions among the majority of the blacks in the country. The "free Mandela" movement gathered worldwide support.

Mandela's following is based on legends of the man and indirect knowledge of his views. It is a crime to distribute any of his writings in South Africa. Once he was known as a spellbinding orator, but the vast majority of his followers today could never have heard him. Even leaders who were formerly regarded by the government as "moderate" now endorse Mandela and the outlawed ANC. Bishop Tutu said, "The government has to come to terms with the fact that the black community now says, 'Our leader is Nelson Mandela and any other persons are just filling in.'"

In January 1985, South Africa's President Pieter W. Botha announced that the government would be willing to release Mandela if he gave a commitment to renounce violence unconditionally. Winnie and her lawyer were allowed to visit Nelson (in Pollsmoor Prison, to which he had been moved in 1982) to get his response.

He dictated a message, which his daughter Zindzi read to a UDF gathering in Soweto on February 10. She said, "My father says, 'I am surprised at the conditions that the government wants to impose on me. I am not a violent man. My colleagues and I wrote in 1952 to Malan [Daniel Malan, then prime minister] asking for a round table conference to find a solution to the problems of our country but that was ignored.'"

He recounted the offers that had been made to succeeding governments. All had been ignored.

It was only then when all other forms of resistance were no longer open to us that we turned to armed struggle. Let Botha show that he is different. . . . Let *him* renounce violence. Let him say that he will dismantle apartheid. Let him unban the people's organization, the African National Congress. Let him free all who have been imprisoned, banished or exiled for their opposition to apartheid. Let him guarantee free political activity so that the people may decide who will govern them.

I cherish my own freedom dearly but I care even more for *your* freedom. Too many have died since I went to prison. ... Not only I have suffered during these long lonely wasted years. I am not less life-loving than you are. But I cannot sell my birthright nor am I prepared to sell the birthright of the people to be free. ... What freedom am I being offered when I may be arrested on a pass offense? What freedom am I being offered to live my life as a family with my dear wife who remains in banishment in Brand-fort? What freedom am I being offered when I must ask for permission to live in an urban area? What freedom am I being offered when I need a stamp in my pass to seek work? What freedom am I being offered when my very South African citizenship is not respected?

Only free men can negotiate. Prisoners cannot enter into contracts. ... I cannot and will not give any undertaking at a time when I and you, the people, are not free. Your freedom and mine cannot be separated. I *will* return.

And so the struggle went on. The illegal ANC flag was draped over the coffins of men, women, and children who had been killed by government police who entered black areas in armored cars. Nelson in prison was only a symbol that the nation was itself a prison for all blacks.

To counter reports that Nelson's health had deteriorated because of prison conditions, the government allowed a visit in 1985 by Conservative British politician Lord Bethell. Bethell compared Nelson to the senior white police officials who were in the room with him: "A tall lean figure with silvering hair, an impeccable olive-green shirt and well-creased navy blue trousers, he could almost have seemed like another general in the South African prison service. Indeed his manner was the most self-assured of them all and he stood out as obviously the senior man in the room. He was, however, black. And he was a prisoner, perhaps the most famous in the world, the man they write songs about in Europe and name streets after in London, the leader of the African National Congress, a body dedicated to the destruction of the apartheid system, if necessary by force."

Later in the year, he had another visitor: American lawyer Samuel Dash, who had been the chief counsel to the Senate Watergate committee. Dash, too, noted the crisp, well-fitted clothing that Nelson wore and the way the guards had of treating him "as though he were their superior, unlocking gates and opening doors on his command as he led me on a tour of his building."

Dash asked Nelson what he thought of "suggestions that the government might repeal laws banning interracial marriage, and ease laws that limit black entry into urban areas."

Nelson described these as "pinpricks." He said, "Frankly, it is not my ambition to marry a white woman or to swim in a white pool. The central issue is political equality."

To Dash, Nelson described the three principles of the ANC program: (1) a unified South Africa without artificial "homelands," (2) black representation in the central parliament, and (3) "one man, one vote."

When Dash pointed out that whites feared domination by the black majority if these demands were honored, Nelson said, "Unlike white people anywhere else in Africa, whites in South Africa belong here—this is their home. We want them to live here with us and to share power with us."

Dash discussed the seeming futility of black revolt against the heavily armed South African government. Nelson agreed that the blacks could not win in direct combat. "However," he said, "over time, and with the help of others on our borders, the support of most other nations in the world, and the continued training of our own people, we can make life most miserable for them."

Indeed, there has been a strong international movement to bring economic pressure on the South African government. Groups in the United States have proposed a divestiture program to pressure American business with interests in the country to withdraw their economic cooperation. Others have boycotted South African goods.

Not everyone agrees that these are the best policies. U.S. corporations that have installations in South Africa point out that they provide many good jobs for blacks, and treat all their employees without regard for race. Economic pressure on the country hurts the poorest people—generally blacks—the most.

Moderate black leaders such as Desmond Tutu originally feared that divestiture would hurt blacks more than white South Africans. Recently, however, Bishop Tutu and others have spoken out in favor of international economic sanctions. This has led many South African whites to urge the government to speak with leaders of the ANC. So far nothing has come of this. But it appears clear that the ANC is and will remain for the near future the group with the most popular support within the country. The UDP has adopted many of the same positions as the ANC.

The government released Winnie from her banishment in Brandfort in April 1986. She returned to Soweto and immediately began traveling about, urging groups to take a hard-line policy against the government. In recent years, she has made known her belief that the white South African government is unlikely to be dislodged without violence.

As Nelson has written, the choice of violence is up to the government, which has the weapons and has used them. It seems a triumph of the human spirit that a man who has spent more than twenty years in prison holds the key to the future of a wealthy and powerful nation. Yet the government clearly fears the possibility that Nelson's death in prison will set off full-scale civil war. But if he is released, he may be an even more powerful leader of his people than any the government has faced. Sam Dash remarked on seeing Nelson, "I felt that I was in the presence not of a guerrilla fighter or radical ideologue, but of a head of state." Nelson may yet become the first black head of a racially equal South Africa.

Perhaps the most remarkable aspect of the story of these two people is the way their affection for each other has survived the years of struggle and separation. Nelson wrote Winnie in a letter in 1985: "As I see it, the true significance of marriage lies not only in the mutual love which unites the parties... but also in the faithful support which the parties guarantee—that it will always be there in full measure at crucial moments.

"Your love and support, the raw warmth of your body, the charming children you have given the family, the many friends you have won, the hope of enjoying that love and warmth again, is what life and happiness mean to me."

And Winnie replied, "If life is comprised of the things you enumerate and hold dear, I am lost for words due to the fact that in my own small way life feels a little more monumental, material and demanding of one's innermost soul. That is why the love and warmth that exude from you behind those unkind concrete grey monotonous and cruel walls simply overwhelms me, especially when I think of those who in the name of struggle have been deprived of that love."

BIBLIOGRAPHY

Benson, Mary. *Nelson Mandela: The Man and the Movement*. New York: Norton, 1986. This is the most important biography of Nelson, based on the author's interviews with him and his family.

————*South Africa: The Struggle for a Birthright*. Hammondswood, England: Penguin, 1966.

Hallett, Robin. *Africa since 1875*. Ann Arbor: University of Michigan Press, 1974.

Harrison, David. *The White Tribe of Africa*. Berkeley: University of California Press, 1981. A fascinating study of the reasons why the whites of South Africa have come to be what they are today.

Harrison, Nancy. *Winnie Mandela*. New York: Braziller, 1986. Written by a white South African, this is an inspiring story of Winnie's personal struggle and development as a person.

Lawson, Don. *South Africa*. New York: Franklin Watts, 1986. This well-known writer of books for young people presents a thoughtful and balanced view of the history of South Africa.

Lelyveld, Joseph. *Move Your Shadow.* New York: Times Books, 1985.

Mandela, Nelson. *No Easy Walk to Freedom.* London: Heinemann, 1965.

——*The Struggle Is My Life.* London: International Defence and Aid Fund for Southern Africa, 1978.

Mandela, Winnie. *Part of My Soul Went with Him.* Ed. Anne Benjamin, adapt. Mary Benson. New York: Norton, 1985.

Oliver, Roland, and Anthony Atmore. *Africa Since 1900,* 3rd ed. Cambridge, England: Cambridge University Press, 1981.

Ungar, Sanford J. *Africa: The People and Politics of an Emerging Continent.* New York: Simon & Schuster, 1985.

NOTES

Unless otherwise indicated, references are only to quotations one sentence or more long.

Chapter One

page 9: Nelson Mandela, *The Struggle Is My Life*, p. 207.
page 14: Mary Benson, *Nelson Mandela*, p. 17.
page 21: Mandela, *The Struggle Is My Life*, p. 207.

Chapter Two

page 26: Nelson Mandela, *No Easy Walk to Freedom*, p. 11.
page 27, lines 19–29: Mandela, *The Struggle Is My Life*, p. 17.
pages 27–28: Mandela, *The Struggle Is My Life*, pp. 17–18.
page 31: Mandela, *The Struggle Is My Life*, p. 25.
page 37: Mandela, *No Easy Walk to Freedom*, p. 10.
page 37: Benson, *Nelson Mandela*, p. 46.
page 39: Benson, *Nelson Mandela*, p. 56.

page 40: Mandela, *The Struggle Is My Life*, pp. 50, 54.

Chapter Three

page 42: Mandela, *Part of My Soul Went with Him*, p. 48.

page 43, lines 3–9: Mandela, *Part of My Soul Went with Him*, p. 46.

page 43, lines 12–18: Mandela, *Part of My Soul Went with Him*, p. 46.

page 43, lines 21–26: Mandela, *Part of My Soul Went with Him*, p. 47.

page 45, lines 8–10: Mandela, *Part of My Soul Went with Him*, p. 48.

page 45, lines 19–26: Mandela, *Part of My Soul Went with Him*, p. 51.

page 49: Nancy Harrison, *Winnie Mandela*, p. 47.

Chapter Four

page 52, lines 15–18: Benson, *Winnie Mandela*, p. 46.

page 52, lines 25–26: Mandela, *Part of My Soul Went with Him*, p. 58.

page 52, lines 29–32: Mandela, *Part of My Soul Went with Him*, p. 59.

page 53, lines 1–7: Mandela, *Part of My Soul Went with Him*, p. 59.

page 55, lines 27–35: Harrison, *Winnie Mandela*, p. 63.

page 56, lines 5–8: Benson, *Nelson Mandela*, p. 82.

page 60, lines 17–21: Mandela, *The Struggle Is My Life*, p. 93.

page 60, lines 22–30: Mandela, *The Struggle Is My Life*, p. 93.

pages 60–62: Mandela, *Part of My Soul Went with Him*, p. 68.

page 62, lines 4–10: Mandela, *Part of My Soul Went with Him*, p. 68.

Chapter Five

pages 63–64: Mandela, *Part of My Soul Went with Him*, pp. 71–72.

page 66, lines 8–13: Mandela, *The Struggle Is My Life*, p. 115.

page 66, lines 17–19: Benson, *Nelson Mandela*, p. 101.

page 66, lines 21–25: Mandela, *The Struggle Is My Life*, p. 102.

pages 66–67: Benson, *Nelson Mandela*, p. 103.

page 67, lines 22–23: Benson, *Nelson Mandela*, p. 104.

page 69, lines 5–7: Mandela, *Part of My Soul Went with Him*, p. 72.

page 69, lines 14–23: Mandela, *Part of My Soul Went with Him*, p. 72.

page 69, lines 26–27: Mandela, *Part of My Soul Went with Him*, p. 74.

page 70, lines 6–12: Roland Oliver and Anthony Atmore, *Africa Since 1800*, p. 298.

page 70, lines 21–25: Benson, *Nelson Mandela*, p. 104.

page 71: Benson, *Nelson Mandela*, p. 110.

page 71, lines 17–24: Mandela, *No Easy Walk to Freedom*, p. 121.

pages 71–72: Benson, *Nelson Mandela*, p. 114.

pages 72–74: Mandela, *Part of My Soul Went with Him*, p. 76.

page 74: Mandela, *The Struggle Is My Life*, p. 125.

page 75, lines 5–10: Benson, *Nelson Mandela*, p. 127.

page 75, lines 12–19: Mandela, *The Struggle Is My Life*, pp. 148–149.

page 77, lines 19–24: Benson, *Nelson Mandela*, p. 147.

page 77, lines 30–37: Mandela, *The Struggle Is My Life*, p. 158.

page 78, lines 4–10: Mandela, *The Struggle Is My Life*, p. 160.

page 78, lines 14–21: Benson, *Nelson Mandela*, p. 151.

page 78, lines 26–30: Mandela, *The Struggle Is My Life*, p. 168.

pages 78–79: Mandela, *The Struggle Is My Life*, p. 175.
page 79, lines 27–36: Mandela, *Part of My Soul Went with Him*, p. 82.

Chapter Six

page 80, lines 5–11: Mandela, *Part of My Soul Went with Him*, p. 85.
page 81: Mandela, *Part of My Soul Went with Him*, p. 89.
page 82: Mandela, *Part of My Soul Went with Him*, p. 88.
pages 83–84: Mandela, *The Struggle Is My Life*.
page 87: Harrison, *Winnie Mandela*, p. 118.
page 88, lines 14–17: Harrison, *Winnie Mandela*, pp. 125–126.
page 88, lines 28–29: Mandela, *Part of My Soul Went with Him*.
pages 88–89: Mandela, *Part of My Soul Went with Him*, p. 83.
page 89, lines 18–24: Mandela, *Part of My Soul Went with Him*, p. 97.
page 92: Harrison, *Winnie Mandela*, p. 133.

Chapter Seven

pages 102–104: The poem is from *Black As I Am* (Los Angeles: Guild of Tutors Press of International College, 1978).
page 104, lines 13–19: Mandela, *Part of My Soul Went with Him*, p. 143.
page 104, lines 23–28: Benson, *Nelson Mandela*, pp. 194–195.
page 104, lines 30–32: Mandela, *Part of My Soul Went with Him*, p. 137.
page 110, line 11–14: Mandela, *Part of My Soul Went with Him*, p. 146.

pages 110–111: Mandela, *Part of My Soul Went with Him*, pp. 146–148.

pages 111–112: Benson, *Nelson Mandela*, p. 228.

page 112, lines 13–19: Dash, "A Rare Talk with Nelson Mandela."

page 112, lines 21–23: Dash, "A Rare Talk with Nelson Mandela."

page 112, lines 30–33: Dash, "A Rare Talk with Nelson Mandela."

pages 112–113: Dash, "A Rare Talk with Nelson Mandela."

page 114, lines 2–3: Dash, "A Rare Talk with Nelson Mandela,"

page 114, lines 9–17: Benson, *Nelson Mandela*, pp. 237–238.

page 114, lines 18–26: Mandela, *Part of My Soul Went with Him*, p. 149.

INDEX

Tsukudu, Adelaide, 49, 52
Tswana language, 100
Tutu, Bishop Desmond,
    105, 107, *108*, 110, 113

Umkhonto we Sizwe, 70–
    71, 72, 77–78
Umtata, *13*
Union of South Africa, 9–
    25
    new constitution, 105,
        107
    state of emergency in,
        107
United Democratic Front,
    105
United States corporations,
    113
Universal Declaration of
    Human Rights, 77

Verwoerd, Hendrik, 66
Voting rights, 14, 16, 31

Whites against apartheid,
    24
Witwatersrand, University
    of, 24
Work stoppages, 36
World War I, 10
World War II, 24, 28–29

Xhosa language, 10, 42,
    100

Youth League.
    See African National
    Congress

Zulu Warriors, 17